MEMOIRS
OF OREGON

IN THEIR OWN WORDS

To. Pat
thanks

J Fowler

J. P. "Jim" Fowler

ISBN: 978-0-615-30713-8

Printed in the United States of America by
Maverick Publications • Bend, Oregon

DEDICATION

To Harry, Ruth, Edgar, Helen, Ed, Betty, Katherine and Hugh
and all native born Oregonians.

ACKNOWLEDGEMENTS

My sincere and ever lasting gratitude to Gordon, David, June, Jeannie, Don, Tricia and Mary whom are family members or friends of the wonderful people in this book. Without their help, it would have not been possible for me to complete it.

A special thanks to Sharon Filardo who gave of her time and efforts with the editing, and to my wife Donna, my Mickey, for assisting me in compiling these stories and her simple acts of kindness caring and assisting others all the time asking for nothing in return.

CONTENTS

PROLOGUE

*"History is the witness that testifies
to the passing of time. It illumines reality,
visualizes memory, provides guidance in daily life,
and brings us tidings of antiquity"*
— Ciro 106 BC

I often recall the tales that my Grandfather and Grandmother Fowler told me about life on the Oregon Trail and settling in the fertile Willamette Valley of 'Eden' (Oregon).

Much of that history is gone, gone forever.

When my Aunt Ruth passed away at the age of ninety-seven, I decided to interview true Oregonians born in 'Eden' in the early twentieth century and pass on their life stories. I was very fortunate to be able to hear their accounts of hardship, joy and sorrow.

There has been so much said about our history being "lost," especially of my aunt's generation and the other regular folks who made Oregon and America great. Because of this, I felt that the history of those who went quietly about their lives, building "Eden", should be saved and told. You will note that I asked each of them the same questions and quote them as if they are sitting in your living room, telling you their stories. You will also notice improper grammar. This was intentional in order to keep the stories "in their own words".

As you read these unique memoirs of ordinary people, born and raised in Oregon, keep in mind their generation. In just 100 short years they built more than any other civilization in history.

They experienced World Wars I, II, Korea, Vietnam and the Middle-East conflicts. Some gave of themselves, while others gave their sons, daughters, grandsons or granddaughters, and some did not return home. These true Oregonians suffered through the Great Depression and the uncertainty of a nuclear holocaust.

I have been fortunate to know many of these people. Come to think of it, I don't recall any of them complaining about their lives or the hardships and strife they went through. They just went about their lives, doing their job, working hard, raising good kids and just being good Americans and Oregonians.

Before I begin, I would like to tell you a little about the beautiful state of Oregon, or "Eden", as the early pioneers referred to it. You know, since it rains all the time, most people think Oregon is just one big swamp. A friend of mine calls our rain, "ocean dust" and says 'you don't sun tan in Oregon, you rust."

In reality, Oregon is made up of seven distinct and different areas; the beautiful rugged 361 mile shoreline of the Pacific Ocean and coastal area with sandy, public beaches and numerous rivers and bays; the fertile Willamette Valley where acres and acres of grass seed, Christmas trees and nursery stock grow; the Cascade mountain range with beautiful snow capped Mt. Hood, Mt. Jefferson and Three Sisters mountains towering over forests of Douglas Fir; Central Oregon features over 150 pristine rivers and high lakes teeming with trophy –sized trout and forests of ponderosa pines and juniper. Eastern Oregon is an arid, high desert with the beauty of the painted hills. The Steens Mountains, with the largest continental, geological fault in America, flanks the southeastern corner of the state. Herds of Mule deer and Pronghorn antelope range in an area the size of some states. The Columbia River gorge separates Washington on the north and Oregon on the south and is the only sea-level route through the Cascade range. The 80 mile long gorge has been carved to its 4,000 foot depth by the mighty Columbia

River. Until you have seen Northeastern Oregon, you have not lived. The "Switzerland of Oregon" as some refer to it, is in the Wallowa-Whitman National Forest which covers over two million acres and includes the rugged 9,880 foot Sacagawea Peak and Hells Canyon, the deepest river carved canyon in North America. Last but not least, is Southern Oregon with the beautiful Umpqua River noted for its steelhead fishing and the Rogue River with its deep canyons and world class rapids. And last but not least, Crater Lake, the glistening jewel of Oregon, is located in the southern Cascade mountain range and is the only national park in Oregon. Due to its enormous depth, its deep blue water never freezes.

The following are the major historical events in Oregon:*

1788 Captain Robert Gray sails into Tillamook Bay and is the first white man to set foot in Oregon.

1792 Captain Gray discovers the Columbia River.

1805 Lewis and Clark reach the Pacific Ocean and they explore the Columbia and Willamette River valleys.

1811 John Astor founds Astoria for the Pacific Fur Company.

1818 The occupancy of Oregon is agreed upon by the United States and Great Britain.

1825 John McLaughlin builds Fort Vancouver on the banks of the Columbia River.

1834 Methodist Minister, Jason Lee, starts a mission in the Willamette Valley.

1843 After 900 pioneers arrive in Oregon, a provisional government is established.

1846 The 49th parallel is fixed for the boundary between the United States and Britain (now British Columbia)

1848 Congress establishes the Oregon Territory.

1857 Oregon's Constitution is written.

1859 February 14, 1859 Oregon becomes the 39th state of the United States.

1902 Oregon is the first state to adopt legislation by the citizenship or by the initiative and referendum amendment to its Constitution.

1913 By Executive Order of Governor Oswald West, all Oregon Beaches were declared Public highways.

1930 to 1951 devastating forest fires consumed 355,000 acres of old growth timber in what are now called the "Tillamook Burns".

1938 Bonneville Dam on the Columbia River begins producing power.

1941 Oregon is the first state to require reforestation of state and private forest land which requires two seed trees per acre planted after timber harvest. This law was amended in 1971 for more aggressive forestation and reforestation following harvest.**

During World War II, Portland was a major ship building area with many wartime industries. To house the workers, the temporary city of Vanport was built as a suburb of Portland on the banks of the Columbia River.

On June 21, 1942, a Japanese submarine surfaced off the mouth of the Columbia River and fired seventeen shells at Fort Stevens. At the same time, the Japanese launched numerous incendiary balloons via the jet stream and a small Japanese airplane also dropped firebombs designed to start forest fires in the southern coastal area of Oregon.

1971 Oregon is the first state in the Nation to pass the Oregon Bottle legislation, which requires deposits on soft drink, beer bottles and cans. In 2009, water bottles were added.

With all its beauty, what really makes Oregon and sets it apart, are its people. The heritage of the pioneers who braved the Oregon Trail to have a better life in "Eden" and the influence of the Native Americans, lives today in these native Oregonians whose stories are unique. In reading this you will note that my questions are typed in bold *Italics*. I have also added *"Authors notes"*. These were added for those who may not be familiar with the history or geography of Oregon.

> *"–some people make headlines,*
> *while others make history"*
> — Philip Dewit

Source: *Oregon Blue Book

HARRY P. FOWLER

Born March 3, 1900
Salem, Oregon
Died, October 31, 1985

"Any man can be a father,
it takes someone special to be a dad."
— author unknown

Authors note: *When I first started thinking about this book, I wondered who and where I could locate native Oregonians born in the early nineteen hundreds. Like a bolt, it came to me to begin it with the history of my best friend, my Dad. Sitting in his meager living room or around campfires when we fished or hunted in the beautiful rugged areas of Oregon, I listened to him recall his life in Oregon.*

Harry Phillip Fowler, the second child of Phillip H. Fowler and Mary Brown-Fowler was born March 3, 1900 in the home built by his grandfather in Wheatland, Oregon and grew up on the huge 'ranch' carved out by his father and grandfather.

Dad was five foot eight and weighed one hundred and sixty pounds. He always had a pleasant look on his ruddy face. Even at the age of eighty-five, his sandy colored hair had not turned gray. He worked hard most of his life but was not stooped over and was in good shape for a man his age. He was a quiet man, but as it's been said, 'still waters run deep'. Using common sense, he always thought out every situation or problem before making decisions. In his later years, to the dismay of my mother, he faithfully practiced on is old guitar with dreams of being good at it. On October 31, 1985, he died from the complications of surgery. He was a simple man who loved his family, Oregon and his country. As a kid and now an adult, he taught me many things that I have passed on to my son.

"when you teach your son,
you teach your grandson."
— author unknown

What is the history of the Fowler family?

"My great grandmother, your great, great grandmother was Tabitha Moffatt-Brown and was born May 1, 1780 and died May 5, 1858. She was a widow who started west from Missouri in April of 1846 with her daughter and son, who was my grandfather, Benjamin Brown. My grandfather told me many stories of the hardships on the Oregon Trail. The group had been led over the Applegate cut-off which began in Fort Hall, Idaho and wound 800 miles into Nevada and California and finally to Oregon. They had been duped by the Applegate brothers who assured them that the new cut-off would get them to Portland long before those that had gone down the Columbia River. Unfortunately, the trip took four months, rather than the usual two months down the Columbia. When they ran out of food, the children cried because they had nothing to eat.

Authors note: *Tabitha Brown was honored in 1987 by a resolution of the Oregon Legislature proclaiming her as the official symbol of "Mother" in Oregon and her name is listed in the Oregon capitol building on the walls of the house chamber.*

My grandfather, George A. Fowler was born August 9, 1822 and died in 1889. Grandmother Rachel born September 6, 1825 and died April 4, 1903, left a good life in Missouri for a new one in "Eden" in the spring of 1864 with daughter Martha, sixteen, sons Marcus, fifteen, James, nine and Phillip, four. My uncle James told me that life on the Oregon Trail was long, hard and sometimes dangerous. The children walked most of the way across the plains and in the deep snow of the Rocky Mountains. They traded tobacco to the Indians for bows and arrows. He said that it took six months to the day from the time they left Missouri until the family arrived in Portland, Oregon.

My grandparents Fowler and their family settled in the Chehalem Valley of Oregon, which is southwest of Portland, and farmed the land in the area of where the city of Newberg is. They later moved to the town of Wheatland, twenty miles south of Newberg in the southwest corner of Yamhill County. Wheatland is located on the Willamette River, which at the time was an important shipping point for crops carried on the many steamboats that ran between Portland and Corvallis. Working long and hard, the family cleared the land of huge Douglas Fir trees and planted crops of grain and hops in the rich loam soil.

My grandfather Benjamin Brown married my grandmother Mary Jane (Spoonemore) Brown in 1858. They had three children, Sarah Alice Brown, born Nov. 29, 1858. My mother, Mary Brown- Fowler was born December 1, 1860, and Benjamin Carr Brown born December 28, 1862.My mother was five foot tall in her stocking feet and five foot around. Over the years I watched her dark brown hair, which she always wore in a bun, turn snow white. Her ruddy, round face and deep blue eyes always had a

3

kind smile which radiated kindness. She was very strict with us kids, especially getting our chores and school studying done.

When she called us by our full names, we knew we were in trouble. Even in those days, she wore the pants in the family in raising us kids and keeping Dad under control. Cooking for Sunday supper for all who would drop by, I can still see her happily standing over her wood stove and the wood fired water heater steaming and jumping, ready to blowup.

To mask her short, stubby body, she always wore a long dress she made herself when she went to town or to church. On Sundays when we went to church, she made sure that Dad and us kids wore our 'Sunday best' and had washed behind our ears. During the week around the house she wore long dresses and aprons she made from flower sacks. When she sorted peaches in the orchard, she would wear her older dresses and always donned a sunbonnet. She passed away on November 9, 1940.

My dad, Phillip Heighton Fowler, was born February 6, 1860 and died March 11, 1943. Dad, standing at six feet four and weighing around two hundred-twenty pounds, dwarfed mother. For as long as I can remember, his long thick hair was snow-white. With his distinctive look, standing erect, proudly carrying himself, many people called him 'Colonel'. He had large brown eyes and his weathered face, scarred on the right side when one of his rifles exploded and seared his skin, was constantly tan even in the winter. He always wore long underwear, except in the hot summer, and the wool shirts mother made. They were always buttoned at the top button. I have always been amazed that I never saw him sweat. Walking, he had a grace and stature of a leader and I can still picture him walking proudly through his beloved hop yards and chatting with the city folks picking the crops.

My sister, Anita, was born January 29, 1898 and died May 10, 1964. She married Al Reed, had five kids, and lived in Myrtle Point, Oregon. Al worked as a logger and in the area sawmills.

My sister, Mildred, was born March 12, 1904 and died from the flu during the big flu outbreak, on April 22, 1919. All of my family, except Anita, is buried in Hopewell Oregon at the Hopewell cemetery. Anita is buried in Coos Bay with her husband and son."

Authors note: Harry and Carol Fowler are buried in Salem at the Rest Lawn cemetery.

What is your earliest recollection of your family life?
"I don't remember my grandparents as grandfather George died in 1887 before I was born, and grandmother Rachel passed away in 1903. I do remember the good times when I was young. I would go with my dad when he worked in the fields and once a week we would go to the city (Salem) in a horse-drawn wagon for supplies. It took most of a day and coming back, dad would stop at each of the small stores along the way to visit. Us kids would play with the other kids and pester Dad for candy at each stop. By the time we got home, we would be full and wouldn't eat any supper. Mother would scold Dad for spoiling us. Dad would just nod his head in agreement. The weekly trip continued until I started school and then only in the summer if my chores were done. By that time Dad had purchased trucks and we rode to town in style.

Due to the floods of the river, the house granddad built was on the highest piece of ground in Wheatland. It was a two-story, wooden house built from the trees Granddad cut down. My room was in the attic above the second floor. It had one large window out of which I could see the Willamette River off in the distance. In the summer it was real hot and in the winter very cold. I kept warm using the quilt blankets Mom made out of old clothing, sheets and dresses.

I don't remember the year, but it must've been when I was nine or ten, we had warm, non-stop rain for about a week and you could see the river rising. Dad got his small rowboat and tied it to the attic window. He sat in my room watching the river rise as Mother and us kids carried what meager valuables we had to my bedroom. The water just kept rising 'til Dad told us we had to get out. I looked out the window and saw that the water was lapping at the attic windowsill and the boat floating next to the house. We all got into the boat and Dad rowed us away, eventually reaching the main road between Salem and Dayton. Us kids were scared and Mom calmed us down telling us ''it will be all right.' We stayed with friends until the river went down. When we got home, we found the house full of mud. All of our neighbors helped each other to clean the houses and get things back to normal. Over the years we had to get out of my window two or three times due to the high water.

We had floods almost every year and we would have to get the horses, cows and sheep up to higher ground around the house. In later years, we moved the tractors and trucks up next to the house. Sometimes it looked like a used tractor and truck sales lot with all the livestock standing around as customers. During one of the floods, the river cut a new channel and took a big portion of one of our hop yards with it".

What else do you remember about the weather?

"Dad told me that during one of the biggest floods, I think it was in the early 1880's, he and Granddad rowed a boat across the Willamette River from the railroad crossing on Wallace Road right up to the steps of the old Marion Country Courthouse where the new courthouse stands now.

Outside of the floods, the winters seemed to be colder with more snow than we've had lately. When I was a kid I remember that many times the snow would be two to three feet deep.

As a kid, the summers were great on the 'ranch.' Us kids would play in the soft loam soil or swim in the river. I was a regular 'water dog' but almost drowned twice. Your grandfather saved me one time and one of his hired men saved me the other time. I must've gone down three times during the last one. I remember 'seeing the light' before I was pulled from the river.

When I got older, I worked alongside my dad and his hired men, in the hop yards, planting and harvesting the grain and peach orchards. It was a boy's heaven with no worries at all.

We organized a semi-pro baseball team and I played short-stop. On Sundays we'd travel to nearby towns to play the local team. It was great fun with picnic baskets, home-brew and home-made ice cream.

I forget the year, but the sternwheeler I worked on got froze in on the Willamette River just up from the falls, south of Oregon City. The ice was so thick that we walked across the river, cut down fir trees, yarded them across the ice, split them and burned them to fire the steam boiler of the boat.

That same year, the river froze over in Salem. Me and my best friend Bert, drove my Maxwell car across the river on the ice from Edgewater Street to a log dump located on the east-side of the river. The ice groaned and cracked some, but we had some liquid courage so it didn't bother us. I had to back the car up the log dump road as my car didn't have a fuel pump.

In 1937, when we lived in Salem, we had a January snow storm which dumped over three feet of snow on us. The town was paralyzed. I had my dad's Dodge pickup truck and used it to open 'B' street, in front of our house.

We continued to have floods until the dams on the Santiam River were built. Edgewater Street in West Salem would flood with water up to the railroad crossing on Wallace Road. In order to get to downtown Salem, people had to ride special trains over the river on the railroad bridge.

The winters of 1950-1951 were very cold with high winds and a couple of 'silver thaws' (ice storms). The ice was real pretty but it brought down many trees, traffic signals, electrical wires and most of the wires and hop poles on the ranch.

The biggest storm we had was the Columbus Day hurricane in 1962 and the only one I'd ever seen. I was working at Capitol

Chevrolet, Cadillac, which at the time was located downtown on Commercial Street. During the height of the storm we watched tree after tree in the Marion Square Park falling on cars and the bandstand. I always parked my car on the west side of Commercial Street and only small limbs and branches fell on it. Your mom worked for the State of Oregon and it took a long time detouring around fallen trees and debris to pick her up. Because of the many fallen trees and downed electrical wires blocking Twentieth Street, we had to park a couple blocks away on Chemeketa Street and carefully walk to our house.

We didn't have electricity or telephones, but since we spent our vacations camping at East Lake each summer we were used to 'roughing it'. I got the gas lanterns and Coleman camp stove going and we had all the comforts. It took over two weeks for Twentieth Street to be cleared and our power put back on, but we survived."

What was school like?

"Well, the one-room school house that my granddad and another farmer built for the town, was located on the road between Salem and Dayton. It was about five miles from our house. I don't remember the teacher's name but she was sure stern with us kids, especially us boys. She was very strict making sure we learned arithmetic and being able to read and write. She would have us spend hours practicing our penmanship, drawing circles and straight lines, over and over again. Living in a small house behind the school, she would spend her Sundays going to church and having dinner with the families of the town. Us kids really had to be on our good behavior when she ate with us. If not, we would be in trouble come Monday at school.

When I was six I walked to school with my sister Anita, who was eight and later with my younger sister Mildred. When I got older, me and the other boys walked together to school, most of the time pestering the girls. During recess we would play stickball and baseball. They were good years, but at the time I didn't think so. I wanted to work with my Dad and just have fun.

The school only went to the eighth grade and if I wanted to go on, I would have to go to school in McMinnville. I thought that schooling was a waste of time as all I wanted to do was be a farmer like my Dad. Boy was I wrong."

You mentioned your sister Mildred. You don't talk about her much. What happened to her?

"Mildred was my younger sister; she was four years younger than me and somewhat frail. She was always catching cold and being sick. She was good at school and wanted to be a nurse or a teacher. Living at home with us she helped Mom around the house and in the peach orchards. She come down sick during the big outbreak of the flu in the winter of 1918. She couldn't fight it off and died in the spring of 1919.

She liked kids and helping people, and would've been a good a nurse or teacher. It took Mom a long time to get over her passin' and for a long time Dad was not himself. Losing one of your kids must be real hard."

When did you see your first car and when did you first drive one?

The first car I saw must've been when Dad and me went to Salem for our weekly shopping trips. I don't remember the kind it was but it sure looked good to me. With all the noise the cars made our horses went crazy. Because of that, Dad would stable them in the horse barn located at the east end of the bridge near the bank of the river.

We had lots of money since the crops were fetchin' good dollars. If I remember right, Dad bought a model A ford in 1910 and it was the first car in Wheatland. At first, Dad just let me sit in the Ford. When I was eleven or twelve, and could reach the pedals, Dad taught me how to drive. The only place Dad let me drive was on the dirt roads of Wheatland and back and forth to the hop fields located about five miles from our house. My mom never learned to drive the new 'contraption' as she called them.

Before prohibition and the great depression, money just seemed to flow. We had bumper crops and the prices were real good. Life was good. From the time I was sixteen until I was thirty-five I must've had a new car every year, from Ford's model T's, to a Model A in 1919. In 1925 I changed to Maxwell's then Hudson's and Cord's. In 1935, just before you were born, I purchased a brand new Chevy four-door sedan. Due to the Depression and World War II, we kept it until the war was over."

Did you serve in World War I?

"Well, the Great-War as it was called, began in 1914 with the United States getting into it in 1917. I was too young at first. We read and heard on the wireless (radio) about our boys and how the war was going. The news of gas attacks and what it did to our boys was terrible. On November 10, 1918, me and one of my friends were ordered to show up in McMinnville to go into the Army. When we got there, we were told to sit down and that they'd get to us soon. While we was waiting, I got to talkin' to a fella named Frank who lived on the outskirts of Salem. About an hour later a lady came out and told us to go home as they wouldn't be needing us as the War was over and the armistice would be signed on November 11, 1918. Boy was we glad.

When we got home I thought Mom would jump out of her skin as she was so happy I didn't have to go and the War was over. I lost track of Frank. I found out he got married, moved to Portland and was a mechanic at a Ford dealership. We were re-aquatinted in 1956 during Donna's and your wedding rehearsal party at Schatic's Chateau restaurant. It turned out that Frank would be your new father-in-law. Frank and I had so much in common, from farming to cars, and as you know, became very good friends."

Did you know of anyone who served in World War I?

"Yeah, two of my brothers-in-law, Art Johnson was in the Navy and Jim Turnbull was in the Army and saw bad combat and was gassed with mustard gas. Another fella came through not long after the war ended wanting a job. I thought he was kinda goofy in the head. He told my Dad that he was in the Great War and that he had been gassed with nerve gas. Dad hired him to do odd jobs around the ranch. We built him a place to stay in a grove of fir trees near the hop yard. I never knew his name. He loved dogs and his dogs, and any stray that came around, lived with him in his shack. I just called him 'the dog man'. Mom would make sure he had something to eat and we had him join us for Thanksgiving and Christmas.

Did prohibition affect you and your family?

"It went into effect in1920, and thankfully, it was repealed in 1933. Outside of trying to take liquor away from us, it really had an impact on my family. Our main crops were hops, and they were used in makin' beer. With prohibition, the need for hops was nil. We couldn't sell any and lost the money we spent the summer before drying and bailing them. With no money coming in we had to pull in our horns. There was no high living for me. No more big cars. For the first time, I had to find a job.

I worked on the steamboats that went up and down the Willamette to help make ends meet. We didn't starve but times were tough. Little did we know things would get a lot tougher.

I honestly think prohibition made criminals out of ordinary people who just wanted to have a good time. I believe it caused people to drink more and I saw many of my friends become alcoholics.

We had to be real careful and sneak around, but we had the crops to make liquor so we always had it. A friend of mine who owned a hardware store in Salem told me that he had never sold so many fruit jars as he did during prohibition. Sowing our oats with friends, taking our own special mix of 'hooch', I had great times going to the various dances around the valley. We really liked the dances held at the Schindler barn.

In 1922 I purchased a brand new Maxwell car. One day I loaded some hooch in the trunk of the car and took off to pick up my best friend Bert Simpson in Salem. It was real hot, so we decided to cool off in the pool hall located on State Street across from the Ladd and Bush Bank. In those days, you backed your car in, at an angle to park. Forgetting about the booze in the trunk, we spent most of the afternoon shooting pool. When we walked back to my car, we saw that a cop was looking at the back of it and liquid was dripping out. We kept walking and went back into the pool hall until the cop finally gave up. When he left, we got in the car and carefully drove off. Outside of wasting a lot of good Booze, we could've gotten into a lot of trouble.

During the summer of 1932, we anticipated that prohibition would be repealed and we planted hops and grain. We guessed right and it was repealed in 1933 and both hops and grain was in big demand again and we got big money for them, the most we ever got. To meet the demand for hops, Dad got a loan from a bank and built several new hops dryers. The good times rolled again for the Fowlers."

How did the Great Depression affect you and your family?

"Like I said, in 1933, due to the big market for grain and hops, we had great times. I had my big cars and lots of money. Things were good. In December 1933, during the heart of the Great Depression your mother and I got married. We purchased fine furniture and appliances for our new home in Salem. I drove each day to Wheatland to help Dad run the ranch.

It seemed like it was overnight when the contracts we had for grain and hops were canceled. With nobody wanting to buy our crops, we just let them rot in the fields. We did thrash some of the wheat for flour and dried a few bales of hops for home-brew. What we didn't use, we gave away and Dad traded some flour and peaches for gas at a service station on Wallace Road.

With no money coming in, Dad couldn't pay the property taxes on the ranch and the mortgage he took to build the hop dryers. We lost the biggest hop yard we had. I was out of work and the worst was yet to come.

The Civilian Conservation Corps, or C.C.C., was developed by President Roosevelt to put men to work building roads, bridges and projects around the country. With my experience operating farm equipment, surveying and the arithmetic boned into my head by my teacher, I was able to sign on with the CCC and worked on projects in Salem, the Oregon coast and Mount Hood. It put food on the table, but more importantly, it gave each of us hope and self respect as we were working for our money and not getting a hand-out.

Banks were failing right and left and Mom and Dad didn't trust them. Mom hid what money they had, mostly gold coins, all over the house, in the barns, even the chicken coop. After she died, we had to tear them apart to find it and I'm not sure if we found all of it.

We always had food as we raised what we needed and gave the extra vegetables, eggs, chicken and milk to other families worse off than us. Every day, your Mom and Grandmother Fowler would give a meal to someone who came to our door hungry."

You said you married in 1933, how did you and Mom meet?

"Well, let's see. It was in 1932 at the Fourth of July celebration on the river. My best friend, Bert Simpson, was going with Ruth Reynolds and they set up a blind date for me with one of Ruth's sisters. I found out later that Ruth's nickname was 'Babe'. I had just finished building an eighteen-foot run-about boat. It was white with natural mahogany trim and had an inboard motor I took out of one of my Dad's old trucks. Bert met me at the ranch and we took off up the river to meet our dates. Ruth introduced me to her sister, Carol, and it was love at first sight on my part. Carol, your mother, was seven years younger than me. She was very shy, reserved but very polite. Shaking her hand, I

13

couldn't take my eyes off her. She was five foot five and looked like she weighed around one hundred twenty, or so. She had a very trim, well, proportioned figure. Her coal black hair was worn in the style of the thirties. Her face, with just a small amount of makeup and lipstick, accented her dancing, green eyes and ever present smile. Sitting around a wooden picnic table, we made small talk and got to know each other. Like me, she grew up on a farm that was located about five miles south of Independence.

We spent the day cruising the river, jumping waves and just having a good time. Ruth and Carol had prepared a picnic lunch of fried chicken and potato salad. Sitting on a blanket near the river we ate our lunch and listened to a band play patriotic music. Besides your Mom being good looking, she was a good cook.

At dusk we got in the boat, anchored in the river and watched the fireworks. Exactly at ten, the girl's big brother was there to take them home.

On the way back down the river, I had a hard time keeping my mind off of Carol. A couple of times Bert had to yell at me to miss sand bars. When we docked the boat in Wheatland, Bert thanked me for the day. Shaking his hand, I thanked him for setting up the date and introducing me to Carol. Bert winked, smiled and said, 'I think you're hooked.' He was sure right, I was hooked real good. Your Mom and me courted for over a year going to dances, driving to the beach, cruising the river and just having a great time together and were married, December 2, 1933."

What do you remember about Pearl Harbor?

"In 1941, we (you, your Mom and me) lived in Salem and each Sunday morning we would drive to Wheatland and have dinner with your grandfather who was now living alone. Your Mother would cook dinner and make sure he had something to eat during the week.

In those days most cars didn't have radios so we knew nothing about it. When we drove into Wheatland, around nine in the morning, on the Day of Infamy, December 7th, 1941, as President Roosevelt called it, we were caught by surprise when one of my friends rushed up to us and told us that the Japs had bombed Pearl Harbor. We drove up to Dad's place and saw that the men were loading their cars and trucks with their guns, bedding, groceries and food the women had fixed. Dad was loading his bedroll into one of the neighbor's trucks. When he saw me, he ran up shouting over the noise, 'the Japs snuck in and bombed our ships at Pearl Harbor Hawaii. It just came in on the radio. The Japs are goin' to land at the coast. We're all gonna stop 'em at the beach. Get your guns; you're goin' with us to stop 'em.'

I rushed into the house, changed out of my Sunday best suit, got my stuff, grabbed my 30.06 rifle, kissed you and your mother goodbye and we headed off to stop the Japs from landing on the beach at Taft. I'm not sure most of the men knew where Pearl Harbor was, but they were going to protect their country. Looking back at the sight of Wheatland that morning reminds me of a very active ant farm.

There must've been over forty of us, including the 'dog man'. Most of the old cars and trucks broke down and it took the rest of the day just to get to what is now the burg of Otis. We spent the night in a barn owned by Walt, a friend of my dad. The next morning, Walt's wife cooked us a big breakfast. As we were about to leave, we were joined by some loggers and the other farmers in the area.

Arriving in Taft, we set up camp and spent the time waiting for the Japs, standing watch and patrolling the beach for the invasion that never came. Other than our makeshift army the only guy we ever saw with a gun was the local sheriff. He'd spend evenings with us, having a drink or two of our 'white lightnin'. We were there for four or five days when he told us to go home, that the Japs were not coming. Disappointed, we packed up and headed home not knowing what to expect in the days ahead."

Did you serve in World War II?

"After the Japs bombed Pearl Harbor I tried to enlist but was told by a sergeant at the induction center that "war is a young man's game". I was forty-one, married and had a child. By the time the war ended I was forty-five so I was not fortunate enough to be able to serve our country. In a way I did serve. With my experience from the three C's, I started surveying for the corps of engineers at Camp Adair, a new army base being built just south of Monmouth. Later I secured a good job with the Parker-Schram Construction Company which was a major contractor building Army bases all over the Northwest.

I was sent to Mountain Home, Idaho to begin the preliminary construction of an air base that was being built especially for the new B-29 Superfortress bomber. There was no housing for families in Mountain Home so I had to leave you and your mom with your grandparents Reynolds, in Independence. I took the train from Portland to Boise, Idaho and hitched a ride to Mountain Home. When I arrived, I couldn't believe my eyes. It was right out in the middle of a sage brush, rock covered, dry desert with only one hotel, a gas station and several bars. Checking into the hotel for a room Parker- Schram had reserved for me, I found that the third floor room's beds had wire springs with well-worn mattresses that sagged in the middle. The only thing that held the curtains together was dust and dirt. There was only one bathroom for six rooms. It sure wasn't what I was used to but it was way better than what our servicemen were having.

I met my guys who'd be working for me that evening during dinner in the crowded hotel dining room. The next morning we caught a ride on an old Army bus to the 'air base' and found just a dust bowl and a small travel trailer for my office.

I sure missed you and your mom, but I was able to come home at Christmas and be with you and Mom. You and Mom wrote me letters each week and I would telephone you when I could and write every day. I had to give the letters I wrote to you to the Army MP's to check over before I could mail them to you. The next year the Army brought in several seventeen foot trailer houses for the army and us guys. I was able to get one for us to live in. You and your mother took the train from Portland to Boise which turned out to be carrying men off to war. Your Mother was the only lady on it and Mom said that you had a great time talking to the soldiers.

I picked you and Mom up in a car I borrowed from the Army and drove to our new home. We spent two years in Mountain Home living in a seventeen-foot house trailer.

You had fun playing with the other kids, especially in the summer wading in the small irrigation ditches that ran through the makeshift trailer park. With the other wives of the construction crew, Mom volunteered making bandages for the Army.

Most days, you'd go with me to the air base and you got to see the first B-29 land at the air base. I don't know about you, but I will never forget the sight of the biggest airplane I'd ever seen with its shiny aluminum glistening against the blue sky. It was something. One day, the army MP'S made all of us civilians get inside the 'Quonset Hut' which now was my office, shut the door, and told us not to come out until they said so. We didn't know what was going on, but then we heard the sound of big motors. I picked you up and set you on my desk and we watched the B-29 land through the window the MP'S forgot to shut. The beautiful plane taxied just past the window. When I saw the size of it, I realized why the concrete in the runway was so deep and heavily reinforced.

Finishing the job at the end of the war I continued to work for Parker-Schram at various jobs in Oregon ending up surveying and managing the construction of a power line from Roseburg to Coquille. During the job we lived in Myrtle Point. You attended the fourth grade and had fun playing with your cousins. The 73 mile long power line went through rugged country covered with old growth Douglas Fir and Myrtlewood trees. We did not have any chain saws or power equipment. The men cut down the big trees with old fashioned, two-man cross cut saws muscle and sweat. It was hard work. Most of the ground was covered with Poison Oak bushes with trunks six inches around. We burned everything, including the Myrtlewood. The smoke from burning the Poison Oak gave every one of us Poison Oak rash from head to toe.

Did anyone in your family serve in World War II?

"Yeah, my nephew, Harold Reed, one of my sister's sons. He lived in Myrtle Point with his mom, dad, brothers and sisters. In the summers he lived and worked on the ranch with Mom and Dad. He was very handy building things and during the summer of 1940, he spent his Sundays building a wood walk-way from the house to the outhouse for his grandparents. In November, Mom slipped on the wet wooden walk and broke her hip. Dad rushed her to the hospital in Salem. The doctors 'set' her hip but she did not get better. Finally the doctors told Dad that gangrene had set in and there was nothing they could do for her. She passed away with Dad holding her hand. Harold blamed himself for building the wood walkway and Dad never got over the loss of Mom. Dad sued the doctors and hospital but lost. Paying off the hospital, doctor and lawyer's bills, Dad lost the rest of the ranch. He was able to live in the home as a caretaker when the bank foreclosed.

Harold was a big, strapping kid. Just after Pearl Harbor when he was only sixteen he enlisted in the Marines. I think he 'fudged' on his age to get in. After his 'boot training', he was able to come home and on his way back to California he stopped by Wheatland for a short time to visit with us.

In August 1944, we received a phone call from my sister who told us that Harold had been killed when the Marines landed on Saipan, a Jap held island located in the South Pacific.

The next day, we drove to Myrtle Point with Dad to be with my sister and family. We attended the small memorial service for Harold. When his remains got home after the war, a full military funeral was held for him. Over the years, my sister continued to proudly display the Gold Star Flag in her front window to honor Harold. Unfortunately too many mothers received Gold Star Flags. To Mothers, the Gold Star Flag represented their Sons who made the ultimate sacrifice, the defense of freedom and America. During the World Wars, many windows displayed several Mother's Gold Star Flags.

What events in Oregon history do you recall?

In May 1948 we had heavy rain for about two weeks steady. The deep winter snow pack was melting real fast and the rivers were bank full. In those days, Memorial Day was the last Monday in May. The weather report for the three day weekend said it would be sunny and warm. We (you, your friend Bob, Mom and me) packed up our camping gear in the new boat I had built that winter and took off that Saturday for Suttle Lake, located just west of Sisters. We no more than got our tents and camp set up when it started to rain hard. To keep the water from running into our tents, you and Bob, like good Boy Scouts, dug trenches around the outside of the tents. The rain stopped that afternoon and we fished until dark, catching three or four nice Rainbows. On Sunday and Monday, the weather turned hot and windy and we battled the waves of the big lake but still caught our limits of big fish.

When we returned home one of our neighbors came over and told us that the City of Vanport had been flooded when one of the dikes on the Columbia River broke. Vanport was a temporary town located just north of Portland and was built during the war to house the shipyard workers. During the height of the war, it was Oregon's second largest city. After the war, servicemen returning from the war lived there with their families when they went to college. The town was wiped out and all those living there were homeless. Fortunately, the flood happened on a holiday, very few lives were lost.

I mentioned the time we thought the Japanese would land at the coast just after they bombed Pearl Harbor and us guys went to Taft to stop them. You know, the Japs tried to start forest fires which would hinder our war effort. Using the jet-stream wind, they sent hot air balloons with fire bombs and a small plane dropped fire bombs in Southern Oregon. Fortunately because of the heavy rain that spring, very little damage was done. After the war a family was killed when they found one the bombs.

On June 21, 1942 a Jap submarine surfaced off the mouth of the Columbia River and fired on Fort Stevens, an Army base located near Astoria. Because of the construction of the con-crete bunkers housing the big coast artillery guns, the guns were unable to depress low enough to return the fire.

What do you love about Oregon?

"First off, the people. Those born in Oregon and most of the transplants are hard working and love our state. Oregonians are very helpful and jump in to help others in time of need asking for nothing in return. You know, the early pioneers referred to Oregon as 'Eden' and in my opinion, it is 'Eden'. We have the beauty of the coast, the Cascade Mountains of Hood, Jefferson and the Three Sisters. The high lakes in Central Oregon are packed with fish and the high desert to hunt Mule Deer and Antelope. You asked about the weather. Winters in the eastern and mid-western states are very cold with heavy snow. The only blizzards and sub-zero temperatures we have are in the moun-tains and sometimes in eastern Oregon.

The southern states have high humidity and damaging hurri-canes each year. Tornado's in 'tornado alley' destroys lives, cities, and towns yearly. Oh sure it rains in Oregon, that's what makes Oregon green. You know most people east of the Rockies think Oregon is just one big swamp, they don't know that three fourths of Oregon is semi or arid desert.

We've only had one hurricane and to my knowledge never had twisters like they have back east. On the Oregon coastline and in the Willamette Valley, the summers are sunny and pleasant with low humidity, gentle ocean breezes and temperatures rarely above one hundred degrees. The winters are mild with only an occasional cold snap and snow. The rest of the state has warm summers, low humidity and cool winters. Southern Oregon is a fisherman's and rafter's paradise in the Rogue and Umpqua rivers. Then there's my favorite place, Crater Lake. I always marvel at its deep blue, rugged shore line. Oregon is still 'Eden' and a great place. I love it all!"

What milestones do you reflect on?
"Milestones, well let's see:
– The good life I had on the ranch.
– The fun times as a kid.
– The many fine cars and boats I had.
– The death of my sister Mildred.
– The two happiest days of my life, when I married your Mom and the day you were born.
– The Depression, Pearl Harbor and World War II.
– The death of Harold.
– The death of your Grandmother and Grandfather Fowler.
– The assassination of President Kennedy.
– The birth or our grandkids, Dan and Lori and our great grandkids."

"Dad, your guiding hand on my shoulder will remain with me forever."
— author unknown

L. RUTH 'BABE' SIMPSON

Born August 15, 1910
Buena Vista, Oregon
Died October 20, 2007

"other things may change,
but we start and end with family"
— author unknown

Ruth, or 'Babe', as I always knew her, was my Aunt on my Mothers side and the last of the Reynolds family. Her mind was "sharp as a tack" and she could remember bygone years like they were yesterday. Sometimes she lived in the past and like with my Dad, I spent many hours listening to her remembering her parents, brothers, sisters and her husband.

She was very reserved and somewhat bashful, but once she got to know you she was your friend for life.

Unable to have children, Babe's life centered on her husband Bert, her parents, brothers and sisters and she was able to enjoy four generations of her nephews and their families.

'Babe' and Bert, rented a house in Salem in 1934 and she continued to live there after his death. The house came up for sale in 1967 and I was able to help her purchase it. She kept the house and yard neat as a pin with nothing out of place and cherished a large Japanese cherry tree in the front yard.

In 2006 she fell, and for at least two days was unable to get up and couldn't reach the telephone. She lay on the floor until one of her great nephews found her. Prior to her fall, we tried several times to get her to wear a medical alert watch. She didn't want one as 'they were for old people'. Recuperating in the hospital, her doctor strongly recommended that she should not live alone. Reluctantly, her Nephews and families heeded the doctor's advice and moved her to an assisted living complex.

When listing her house for sale to have money for her care, my cousin David said, 'it was the most difficult decision I ever made'. We were able to use most of her fine furniture in the unit that had a small kitchenette, a good size living, bedroom and a handicap bathroom. At first aunt 'Babe', hated it, but later asked us, 'why we hadn't moved her sooner' and said, 'I just love this place. It's so nice'.

Before she died she recalled her family and life-long friends who had passed away. She often said, ' You know, all my friends are gone. Thank God I have you kids'. She lost her precious wedding rings and we searched her apartment top to bottom. Unable to find them, she became heartbroken, pulled into herself and was never the same. It's my opinion that Aunt 'Babe' didn't want to live after the death of Uncle Bert and then losing the last reminder of him, she couldn't wait to join him in heaven. Her wish came true on October 20, 2007, when she peacefully passed away.

The following memoirs are recollections of conversations Aunt 'Babe', my cousin Gordon, and myself had over the years. Aunt 'Babe' was about five foot five and had the full figure of her English ancestors. Her light brown, almost blond hair was al-

ways neat, and in the style of the times. Wearing stylish eye glasses, her round face was accented with just a hint of make up.

What is the history of your family?

"Oh my, I really do not remember my grandparents Reynolds. I was told that they migrated from England to Mapleton, Iowa but I do not know what year. My father, James A. Reynolds was born December 21, 1869 in Iowa and died, December 19, 1961. My mother, Minerva Schrunk-Reynolds was born August 28, 1875 in Iowa and died, September 21, 1963.

Mama and Dad were married December 25, 1895. They lived in Mapleton Iowa until the spring of 1905 when they moved by train to Salem, Oregon with their family, Gladys, age 8, Harold Age 6; Cyril ('Mike') age 5, and Marjorie, age 2.

My grandfather Schrunk's family came to America from England and settled in Mapleton Iowa. He and my grandmother moved to Oregon in the late eighteen hundreds and lived in Salem. I don't know what he did to make a living but was very wealthy and owned several large homes located on Thirteenth, and Fourteenth streets, between Center and Marion streets. They are still there, but over the years they have been remodeled many times.

Living in one of the houses when they arrived in Salem, Dad worked for grandfather Schrunk until 1907 when grandfather Schrunk helped Mama and Dad purchase a 400-acre farm located about five miles south of Independence. The farm was in the Buena Vista area and had a large, two story home, with four bedrooms and one bathroom located on the second floor. In December of 1907, my sister Carol was born and I came along in 1910. Being the baby of the family is how I got my nickname, 'Babe'. I liked it better than my given name, Luella, but sometimes I think people thought I was named after Paul Bunyan's big blue ox, 'Babe.'"

My sister, Gladys, married Jim Turnbull and had one son, David. For awhile, they lived in Portland when Jim owned a small grocery store. Moving back to Salem, Jim worked for the State of Oregon Secretary of State's office. During the war, Gladys was in charge of the Farm Labor Office and organized 'crop picking platoons' that picked farm crops in the summer. I was a platoon leader for many years and enjoyed being with the teenagers. After the War, Gladys was in charge of the home economics department at The Oregon State Fair where she started the 'Queen of the Kitchen' program. She also served as executive secretary of the Marion–Polk County unit of the American Cancer Society. Gladys died January 14, 1973 and Jim passed away on July 10, 1981.

Brother Harold married Mary Hamilton and had one son, Dick. Harold worked for several Ford dealerships in the Parts departments and was manager of the Parts departments of Valley Ford in Salem, and Phillipi Ford in Stayton. Just after I graduated high school, Harold got a part time job for me driving new Fords from Portland to the dealerships in Salem and Independence. Harold was the type who paid attention to every detail and everything was neat as a pin. He started collecting wood pencils when he was very young and continued to do so until his death. He must've had a thousand of them. I don't know whatever happened to them. I think they would be very valuable now.

Mary was a Registered Nurse and worked in hospitals in Salem and Stayton. After Harold and Mary retired, they managed the Wagontire Oregon store and motel located on Highway 395 between Burns and Lakeview in the high desert of eastern Oregon. Harold and Mary retired to the Willamette Valley after spending a couple of years at Wagontire. Harold passed away on March 17, 1984 and Mary died on April 6, 1973.

My sister Marjorie married Art Johnson and had one son, Gordon. Marjorie was the musician in our family playing the piano. She played for silent motion pictures at the movie theater in Independence. Marjorie and sister, Carol, sang on a talent program on the KEX radio station in Portland. She could play every kind of music and knew the words to most of the songs she played. Our families spent many enjoyable hours listening to her play and singing along with her. Both Marjorie and Art were very active in Post 9 of the American Legion in Salem. Art was a Past Commander and Marjorie was past president of the Auxiliary. Marjorie worked in Salem at Miller's Department Store, State Street Variety, and Woolworth's and the Tax Division of the State of Oregon. Art worked for the Oregon State Highway division until he retired. Marjorie lived to be one hundred and one. Art died on January 15, 1965.

Brother 'Mike' was a confirmed bachelor. For many years he always said, 'after living with us girls, no other girl was good enough for him.' He worked at various jobs and retired from the Oregon Highway Department as a Weigh-master on Highway 6, just outside of Tillamook. Mike was the kind of guy who never met a stranger. He always had a smile on his large face and a joke for us to laugh at. Even with just one leg, and in his later years battling cancer, he was always joyful and mischievous. He loved kids, especially you and your cousins.

While living in Tillamook, he finally found a girl good enough for him, and married Illa Davidson. Illa was a legal secretary for a big law firm in Tillamook. Illa was about four foot eleven standing on her tip-toes and weighed about one hundred pounds. I still remember her digging razor clams at the beach. She'd reach down into the hole she dug in the sand to get the clam, and all you could see was her legs sticking out of the hole. Always with a Pell Mell cigarette in her mouth, and a warm and friendly smile on her small face, she brought Mike happiness, especially in his later life. My 'Mike' died on April 21, 1961 and Illa passed away, November 4, 1982.

Sister Carol, your mom, married Harry Fowler and had one son, you Jim. Carol worked in Salem for Miller's Department store, Woolworth's and the Oregon State Tax and the Highway Department until she was incapacitated from a cerebral hemorrhage in 1967. Your Mom was an accomplished cook, especially meat. She would cook pot roast like no other. She was also a very good writer, I guess that's where you get your writing ability from. Carol sang and Marjorie played the piano in a small band that entertained at dances held by fraternal and civic clubs. I'm sure you remember her "Goop Burger" stand she had at the Oregon State Fair for three years in the early 1950's. She must've made over 200 gallons of her famous Goop Burgers. Goop Burgers was her own secret recipe and was made of hamburger, chili and tomato sauce and who knows what, She served them on a hot dog bun. I can still taste them.

Harry worked on defense projects during the war and until his retirement, worked in Salem as Service Manager of Douglas McKay Chevrolet, Cadillac (now Capitol Chevrolet Cadillac). Your Dad enjoyed the out of doors 'roughing it' in the wilds of Oregon hunting and fishing and was a great 'camp cook'. I remember one trip we took to East Lake. Before we left on the four hour trip, he wrapped a pot roast with carrots and onions and some beer in burlap and put it just behind the radiator of his car. When we got to the lake and had our camp set up, he unwrapped the meat and we enjoyed one of the best meals I've ever eaten.

As you know, he was very active in the Salem Elks Lodge and he told me he was very proud when you were installed as Exalted Ruler (President of the Lodge). Carol passed away in her sleep on September 25, 1994. On October 31, 1985, Harry died from complications of surgery.

Now, all I have left is you, David, Gordon and Dick. I sure wish I could see Dick, but I don't know where he is. You, your cousins and your families, four generations are the family I have left."

What is the earliest recollection of your family life?

"My childhood on the farm was very similar to the TV show, The Waltons. Our large family worked together to make a simple living from the farm. I shared a room with Carol and we played together having a great time.

Dad had two large workhorses and when Dad and Harold were through working the fields in the evenings, Harold would sit me on top of one of the big animals and lead them around the barnyard.

Working with the workhorse, Dad cleared the land of scrub oak trees, planting grain and corn and raised cattle and sheep in the big meadow. Mama planted a large vegetable garden each year. Us girls helped her with the garden and took care of the chickens and pigs.

My brother 'Mike' was just fourteen months old when he got pneumonia. While he was being treated in the hospital, he fell out of his crib, breaking his leg. For some reason gangrene set in and they had to amputate it. He never knew what it was to walk on his own two legs. His chores around the farm were milking the two cows and helping Dad and Harold as best he could on his artificial leg. Each year, as 'Mike' grew, Mama would have to take him on the train all the way to Chicago to get a new leg. If you never knew better, you wouldn't know he only had one leg. He played baseball, basketball and rode horses, always smiling and having a good time.

I don't remember how 'Mike' got his nickname, 'Mike'. Mama and Dad always used his given name, Cyril. To us kids and others, he was just 'Mike'. He was the most outgoing of all us and had a magnetic personality. With his ever present optimistic outlook on life he was the kind of guy you wanted to be around. He was very mischievous, always teasing us girls, and kidding his brother, and friends.

He told me one time, when he and Mama were in the doctor's office in Chicago waiting to get a new leg, he was crying and feeling sorry for himself until another young boy came in without any legs. He said he never felt sorry for himself ever again.

Mike contracted cancer in his 'good leg'. For years he battled as a 'guinea-pig' when he received experimental radiation and other treatments. Even with his incurable decease, he still kept his happy outlook on life, never complained and accepted what the good Lord gave him. He died April 21, 1961 and Illa passed on November 4, 1982.

Christmas was special for Mama and Dad as they were married December 25, 1895 in the home of Mama's parents in Mapleton Iowa. The Reverend E.S. Johnson, who went on to be the Methodist Bishop of Africa, conducted the service.

When Dad got good prices for our crops we would take the train to Newport for a week's vacation. We got off the train in the South Beach area and had to take a ferryboat to get to Newport as the bridge across Yaquina Bay, built by the Civilian Conservation Corps, wasn't completed until 1936.

We camped on the beach near Nye Beach and had a great time swimming in the ocean and the Natatorium. Each evening we sat around a roaring campfire and Marjorie, Carol and I sang, entertaining all those around. To give Mama a break from cooking, all of us kids chipped in and did all the cooking. The boys cooked breakfast, we snacked at lunch and us girls cooked our dinners. Mama and Dad sat holding hands watching their family enjoy themselves and the beauty of the Oregon Coast.

Christmas has always been equally important to us as kids and adults. On the farm, Dad and my brothers cut down Christmas-trees that grew on the farm. Us girls would decorate them with homemade ornaments, strings of popcorn, garland, and candles. On Christmas Eve, Dad would light the candles and turn out the lights. With the glow of the candles and the fire in the large fireplace, we would sit around the tree and sing Christmas Carols. Christmas day us younger kids would open one gift and candy from Santa. Until later years, I don't remember Mama or Dad ever receiving a gift.

We went to church in Independence with grandfather and grandmother Schrunk in their big car. After church we enjoyed large Christmas dinners of vegetables grown in our garden and turkeys 'Mike' raised. Keeping with our English tradition, we always had Mama's homemade plum pudding with rum/vanilla sauce.

On Sunday, December 18, 1927, all of our family had gotten together on the farm to celebrate Dad's and Carol's birthdays. While Dad, Harold and Mike cut firewood in the morning, Mama and us girls decorated the Christmas tree. As we always did on Sundays, we had an early dinner in the afternoon and were going to have birthday cake and presents that evening. After the dinner dishes and the kitchen were cleaned up, all of us, except Dad walked down the hill to visit with our neighbors and exchange Christmas gifts. Dad didn't go as he was worn-out from cutting wood all day. He said he was going to take a hot bath and relax by the fireplace.

We were at the neighbors for just a short time when someone shouted that our house was on fire. Running back up the hill in fright, we saw the house was completely on fire. At first, we couldn't find Dad. Running around to the rear of the house, Harold found him, on the ground, in the snow, horribly burned on his back and arms.

Mama and the older kids wrapped Dad with a flannel blanket. I watched my Dad in such terrible pain and had to look away. Mama, Gladys, Harold and Mike loaded Dad in Harold's car and rushed him to the hospital in Salem. I don't remember how Marjorie, Carol and I got to the hospital. I would guess that the neighbor took us.

Dad had third degree burns on his back and for over a month was hospitalized. Later he said when he was in the bathtub, he thought he smelled smoke. He got out of the tub and wrapped a towel around him. Opening the bathroom door, he saw flames shooting up the stairs and the hallway full of smoke and fire. Unable to go down the stairs, he ran through flames in the hall to a back bedroom and jumped out the window. He landed on the roof of the back-porch and fell to the ground with the towel burning around him.

With our house and belongings burned up, we moved to Salem and lived in a furnished house on North Fourteenth Street grandfather Schrunk owned. I don't think Mama and Dad had any fire insurance and with Dad's hospital bills adding up, things didn't look good for us. We received gifts of clothing and house-hold goods from our neighbors in Buena Vista, our Church and friends. We visited Dad every day and celebrated Christmas while he was in the hospital. We had a Christmas tree at our new place. Each of us got a gift, but with our Dad in the hospital, our house and belongings burned up, Christmas 1927 is one none of us will ever forget.

In the spring of 1929, Mama and Dad bought the Landis Court Apartments in La Grande Oregon and moved to begin a new life in the Northeastern Oregon small town. I was the only one of the kids living at home and leaving my brothers, sisters and my friends at Salem High School was very difficult for me. Our time in La Grande was difficult and trying. With the Depression the money from the apartments didn't come in as promised. Mama and Dad sold the place and we moved back to Salem.

With the help of Grandfather Schrunk, Mama and Dad purchased a large house and farm located just south of Chemawa Road on State Route Eight, which is now North River Road in Keizer.

Dad farmed the place raising strawberries, chickens and had two cows. When it got too much for him they sold the place in 1935 during the early part of the Depression. Dad had trouble selling the livestock and farm equipment and was forced to hold an auction, selling most of it at a loss.

That same year, Dad got a job as the caretaker of the Mount Hood estate owned by Fred Meyer (the founder and owner of the Fred Meyer Stores). I'm not sure how Dad found the job, but I would guess it was through Grandfather Schrunk. Mama and Dad lived in a large, mountain style home that had several bed-rooms. The estate had two large swimming pools and was close to several creeks and rivers. I remember when I looked out the kitchen window, I could almost touch the tip of Mount Hood. The Meyers treated Mama and Dad like family and encouraged our family to use the facilities of the estate. In the summers the Reynolds clan enjoyed the pools and nearby forest. In the winter, we had to struggle trough the deep snow on the narrow roads to visit Mama and Dad.

When you were only eighteen months old your Mom, Dad and you were snowed in early in January 1937 when you were visiting Mama and Dad at Mt. Hood. The water pipes for the house and heating boiler froze up. Mike and your dad eventually was able to get them thawed and the broken pipes fixed. Your Mom said it was very cold in the house. To keep you warm one night she put a hot water bottle in your crib. Around three in the morning, you woke up crying. The water bottle had leaked and you were soaking wet.

Taking care of the large estate became too much for Dad and they had to leave Mount Hood. They bought a large two-story house on Sixth Street in Independence. Mama was again near her old friends and Dad became a 'gentleman farmer'.

During World War II, Dad raised chickens and sold them to the Army at Camp Adair located just south of Independence.

Our family would get together to celebrate birthdays, Mothers and Fathers days, Thanksgiving and Christmas. In the summers we would have family picnics in the Dallas City Park. Dad with his four grandsons helping, made home-made ice cream and each one of you took turns licking the old wooden paddle.

As I said, Christmas was always very special even when the family totaled eighteen. Keeping with English tradition, we exchanged gifts on the eve at my sister Gladys' home. On Christmas day we gathered again and enjoyed a family Christmas dinner and Mama's plum pudding."

What do you remember about the weather?

"I remember as a kid on the farm, the summers were hot with long 'Indian Summers' in the Fall. During the winters we had much more snow and cold weather than we now have. I remember walking out to the barn and the snow would be over my head. Dad would hook up the horses to a sleigh and take us to school and to church in Independence. It was real fun.

Some years it would rain all the time, with high wind. Many times at night, hearing the wind blowing hard outside my bedroom, I was sacred to death and covered my head with my blankets. To this day, wind still bothers me. Many years the Willamette River and the small creeks would flood. To get to Salem we had to take a train across the railroad bridge from West Salem.

In La Grande, it was very hot in the summer and in the winter very cold, with deep snow and wind. Dad struggled to keep the furnace working and shoveled the snow from the front porch steps and sidewalk. It was just awful.

When Bert and I lived on 'D' Street, we had several 'silver thaws' which brought down trees and electrical wires.

In January 1937 a snowstorm dumped three feet of snow. It was the deepest we've ever had in Salem. I walked down to your cousin Gordon's and your house, bundled you boys up and pulled you around on a sled. You were just two and Gordon was seven. I don't know who had more fun, me or you boys?

Camping at East Lake in Central Oregon, some summers, it snowed on us with freezing temperature. Bert and I would keep our food and fish cold in snow banks and the water in our water bucket inside our tent would freeze. Other summers it would be very hot and dry with terrible electrical storms and many mornings our boat would be covered with ice, and by noon it would be ninety degrees.

The worst storm we had was, October 12, 1962, the Columbus Day Storm, as it's called. It was a hurricane and came in unexpected with over one hundred mile an hour winds. I was working for Henry Meier Furniture located in Salem above Miller's Department store on the corners of Liberty and Court streets. We watched the traffic signals sway back and forth, and debris flying through the air. I was petrified. The lights went out as we continued to watch the storm.

34

When the wind finally subsided, I walked down Court Street to my car parked behind Judson's Plumbing on Front Street. The sidewalk was covered with all sorts of roofing, glass, papers, and tree limbs. It seemed like it took me forever to get home. D Street was covered with tree limbs and I had to slowly drive around the mess.

Getting home, I found that the electricity was out. I got my flashlight and checked around the house. My precious Japanese cherry was still standing and only a few shingles were missing on the roof. Fortunately it didn't rain much and I was able to get the roof fixed the next day. My Bert had died just six months earlier and I was by myself, scared to death. I spent that night in bed with my head covered. Somehow I got by being alone.

The next day, I walked to my sister Marjorie's house on Imperial Drive and spent the day with them. My lights came back on about two days later. It took weeks for others. I was lucky."

What was school like? Where did you go? Did you graduate? Go to college?

"All of us kids went to school in Buena Vista. It was a very small school with only three rooms for grades 1-6. Mama packed our lunches and made sure we were 'presentable" in our handmade clothing. When the weather was good, we walked the five miles. In bad weather, Dad would take us in the horse drawn wagon or sleigh when it snowed.

I really liked school, from the beginning until La Grande. Mama made each of us study the three 'R's" each night. Our teachers were mostly young women who had just graduated from college in Monmouth. Once a week a lady would come and tell us Bible stories. Each Christmas, the school had a Christmas play. Carol and I sang. Marjorie played the piano and sang with us. The three of us also performed in talent programs on an Albany radio station.

When we lived in Salem, after the fire, I went to school in tenth and eleventh grades at Salem High School. The school was huge and I was just a 'country bumpkin', very bashful and stayed in the background, not taking part in any school activities. My senior year we moved to La Grande and it was just awful. Coming from the school in Salem, I was way ahead of the local kids in my studies. My classmates were unmerciful in teasing and harassing me all the time. I was from the 'big city' and upset their way. I cried myself to sleep many nights, until I just quit school. Mama was very upset and disappointed in me and Dad said that he'd made a big mistake buying the apartments and sold the place at a loss.

We moved back to Salem. I think the reason was he wanted me to finish school. I was very happy in that I would be near my sisters and other friends. I enrolled in Salem Senior High School and graduated with the last class of 1929. The school was located where the Macy's downtown store now is.

Gladys graduated from Oregon State College and Harold, for a short time went to Oregon State. Due to the money Mama and Dad lost on the fire and the apartments in La Grande, the rest of us kids were unable to go on to college."

When did you see your first car? When did you drive your first car? What kind of cars did you have?
"The first car I ever saw was Grandfather and Grandmother Schrunk's when they came to the farm to visit. I don't know what kind it was. I do remember we had fun riding in the back of their big car when they took us to Church or Salem.

I got my first driver's license in 1929. It cost one dollar. In fact, I still have it in my scrapbook. My boyfriend, Bert Simpson, taught me to drive his big car. I think it was a Buick. At the time, I was five foot two and weighed one hundred-fifteen pounds, and had trouble steering the big, heavy thing. Except during the war years, Bert and I had new Buicks every two, or three years.

The last car I bought was a 1968 Buick Skylark coupe. It barely fit in my small garage and I couldn't open the drivers-side door. I had to crawl over the console to get out of it. I quit driving in 1990 and sold it. I really missed having a car and having to rely on others to ferry me around."

How did World War I affect you and your family?

"I really don't remember much about it. My brother Harold was too young at first. If the war would have continued, from what he told me, he would have gone. Brother Mike was too young and with his artificial leg was exempt from it. Our family listened to the news of it on our wireless radio. When the war was over, Mama and Dad took us kids to a big parade in Salem. I'm not sure what the occasion was, but I remember the weather was cold as I watched the soldiers march by."

Did you know anyone who served in World War I?

"My sister Gladys' husband to be, Jim Turnbull, served in the Army and was hurt in hand-to-hand combat with a German soldier and was gassed with mustard gas. Sister Marjorie's husband to be, Art Johnson, served in the Navy."

How did prohibition affect you and your family?

"I don't remember much about it. Dad told me later that he had trouble selling the grain and corn he raised to his regular customers, but had no trouble selling it to people who bought the corn to make their liquor and home brew.

Due to her strict Schrunk upbringing, Mama would not let any liquor in the house. None of the family drank so it didn't bother us. The plum pudding at Christmas did have a small amount of rum in it, but that's all. Mama mellowed some and on special occasions let Dad have a beer. I'm not sure, but I think one of Mama's brothers ran on the Prohibition Party ticket for Vice President of the United States. When I got older, it seemed that every one of my friends had some kind of homemade liquor or beer. It was always around.'"

How did the Great Depression affect you and your family?

"Well, let's see, in 1928 Mama and Dad bought the apartment house in La Grande. The railroad rented rooms for their workers so they had some money. Mama managed the little money that came in and we got by.

Almost every day, hungry people with families would come to our door for something to eat. In the winter, Dad would have them come in the house out of the cold and Mama would always find something for them to eat, saying, 'it's our turn to help others'.

When we moved back to Salem, I worked for a friend of Grandfather Schrunk as an office clerk after I graduated from high school and lived with Mama and Dad in Keizer. Sisters Marjorie and Carol worked at the Woolworth store located on Liberty Street in Salem. My brothers-in-law, Jim and Art worked for the State of Oregon for one dollar a day. Your Dad worked on your grandfathers hop ranch and then surveying for the Civilian Conservation Corps.

Living on the farm in Keizer from 1929 to 1935, Mama and Dad grew all kinds of vegetables and had eggs, milk and meat for us. They continued to help others. From 1935 until 1941, they lived at Mt. Hood and Dad worked for Fred Meyer. He received a good salary and they didn't have to pay rent.

Bert had a job with the Oregon Highway Division making one dollar a day. I worked as a clerk for grandfather Schrunk after I got married in 1932 and throughout the War. We rented our first house from him on north Fourteenth Street and lived there until we rented a larger house at 1470 'D' street in 1934. Somehow, we survived the depression. Looking back at it now, I don't see how."

When and where did you meet Uncle Bert?

"My sister Marjorie's husband, Art Johnson, introduced us at a party they had at their house. We went together for about a year and married December twenty-fourth in 1932. The wedding was held at Mama and Dad's place in Keizer. Your dad and Bert were best friends and your Dad was Bert's best man.

During the 1932 Fourth of July celebration, Bert and I introduced your Mom and Dad to each other. It's a small world, isn't it?

Bert and I were unable to have kids, so you, your cousins, Dick, Gordon and David, are my kids. As you know, my grand nephews and nieces also are my family.

Bert loved to fly fish. Teaching me, we fished together in the Santiam, Crooked, Metolious Rivers, and East Lake. Each winter, Bert would rewrap and refinish our bamboo fly rods.

On March 31, 1962, my life changed forever. Bert was busy getting ready to go to work and I was in our kitchen preparing breakfast. He said he wasn't feeling too good and went in the bathroom. I called him to come and eat. When he didn't come for breakfast, I went to the bathroom and found him on the floor, dying from a heart attack. I didn't know what to do. I called my sister Marjorie who rushed to my house with her husband Art. He took charge of things and with the help of my other brothers-in-law, made all the funeral arrangements. I was devastated and lost. Thank god my brothers and sisters were there when I needed them. Somehow, with their love and comfort, I got through that terrible time. He was my life for over thirty-two years, and he still is. You know, I can still see him lying on the floor as he died. I just can't get that awful sight out of my mind. Many people said that I would get over my loss, but I never did, I never will."

What do you remember about Pearl Harbor?

"Bert and I were sitting in our small kitchen finishing breakfast and reading the Oregon Statesman newspaper when the phone rang. I got up and answered it. My sister Gladys was on the phone. She was very excited, almost shouting, to turn on the radio, the Japs have bombed Pearl Harbor, Hawaii. At first I thought she was kidding me. I finally realized from the sound of her voice that she was serious. I repeated the news to Bert who rushed into our living room and turned on our Philco radio. After talking with Gladys, we sat listening to the radio and looking at a map of the Pacific Ocean.

The next day, we listened to President Roosevelt declaring war on Germany and Japan. We didn't know what to expect. There were rumors flying all over that the Japs were reported landing on the Pacific coast. Your Dad, Grandfather Fowler and many men from the Willamette Valley went to the coast to stop them."

How did World War II affect you and your family?

"From the day the Japs bombed Pearl Harbor until the war was over, our lives changed. There were mandatory blackouts and we had to cover our windows and we couldn't drive at night with the lights on. Air raid sirens were installed in Salem and tested weekly. At night, Air-Raid Wardens and Block Wardens checked each house in their area to make sure light couldn't be seen.

Due to the war effort, everything from meat to gas and tires were rationed. I still have some food rations and gas stamps in my scrapbook. We scrimped on everything and planted 'Victory Vegetable Gardens', saved our cooking grease, oil, tin cans, cardboard and newspapers. To help win the war, we purchased War Bonds with what little money we had. Mama and Dad lived in Independence and with the shortage of gas, we couldn't visit them each Sunday. All of us kids wrote them each week and Mama answered back. We still had our family gatherings on Thanksgiving and Christmas, but were somewhat subdued due to the war.

Many times Bert and I waited at the railroad crossing on 'D' Street for troop trains pulled by large steam engines, to pass.

The cars were full of men going off to war and flatbed railroad cars were loaded with tanks and big guns. The soldiers waved at us leaning out the windows and we waved back. Seeing them, I always wondered to myself, how many of them would return home.

We read and listened to the news of 'D Day' in Europe and the war in the Pacific. Hearing on the radio about dropping the Atom bombs on Japan, it was hard for us to picture the devastation one bomb could do.

On 'VJ Day', (the day Japan surrendered), Art and Marjorie organized a potluck celebration in front of their house on Imperial Drive. Their neighbors, friends and all our family came. The tables were heaped with what food we had and extended the full length of the street. We even had home brew and liquor; it was quite a party. We were all so happy that the war was over and our boys would be coming home"

Did anyone in your family serve in World War II?

"No, my Brother Harold was too old and due to his artificial leg, brother Mike was exempt. My brothers-in-law, Jim, Art and your Dad were also too old to serve and Bert was classified '4-F'. You know, all of them wanted to go and except for Mike, they would have if the war had lasted any longer.

Jim, Art, and Bert served as Block Air-Raid Wardens. They walked around their neighborhoods at night making sure that the houses were blacked out. There were numerous men from Salem in the war and many of them didn't come back. We saw many 'Gold Star Flags' in windows when we walked to work. The only person we knew personally was your cousin, Harold Reed, who was a Marine and killed on Saipan."

What events in Oregon history do you recall?

"I remember when the State Capitol building burned down in 1935. We could see the glow from the fire at our house on D Street and walked down and watched it.

There were several big forest fires called the Tillamook Burn. During one of them, I was visiting my sister Gladys in a Portland hospital after she had given birth to David. The smoke was so thick it blotted out the sun.

This wasn't just about Oregon but it was real scary and affected a lot of people in Oregon. The evening of October 30, 1938, your Mom and Dad had a Halloween party at their house on North Winter Street. We were having a good time, when an Oregon State Policeman, who was one of your neighbors knocked at the door. He was shouting and very excited telling us that the world was coming to an end. He had just heard news reports on the radio that Martians had landed in the East and were killing people right and left. He said he was supposed to go to work, but he was going to get his family and 'head for the hills.'

Your dad turned on your RCA radio and we heard a frantic reporter saying that he saw a Martian with tentacles incinerate the crowd with heat rays. Your Mom grabbed you from your crib and all of us were sure that the Martians were coming. As we listened, the announcer finally said that it was a reenactment of The War of the Worlds and a simulated program. When your dad heard that he ran outside to stop the neighbor but he was already gone. With a sigh of relief, we continued to listen to the program as 'reporters' told us that the New Jersey police had declared Martial Law and attacked the Martians and about the large force of Martians. From time to time, another radio announcer said that the program was just a simulated program and not real, but if you didn't hear that, the program was so real you would believe that Martians had landed.

When the program continued, it told about the Martians invading and obliterating the Army and 'news reports' of damage, evacuations and that the Martians had destroyed power stations, bridges and railroads. There was the sound of coughing and the 'reporter' stopped talking right after he told about thick black smoke.

The next day, the newspaper reported that thousands of people all over the United States panicked and fled their homes in fear and hid in their cellars, loaded their guns and wrapped their heads with towels to protect themselves from the Martian poison gas. It was also reported that some peopled committed suicide.

During World War II a Jap sub shelled Fort Stevens near Astoria and again rumors were flying around about the Japs invading the beach at Seaside.

On Memorial Day 1948 the town of Vanport was destroyed by a flood when a dike on the Columbia River gave way. All the people were homeless but not many drowned. The next day, Bert had to be in Portland on business, so I rode with him and we saw the devastation of the war-time town. It was just awful."

What do you love about Oregon?

"The beauty of it and its people. You know Bert and I would drive to the beach just to watch the beautiful sunsets. Our favorite place was the Metolious River located in Central Oregon, near Black Butte. We would leave Friday night just after Bert got off work and drive to the river. We set up our camp and fly fished Saturday and Sunday. Even in those days, we would keep just a few fish and then "catch & release' the rest. You know, the Metolious just seems to jump out from the ground at the base of Black Butte. In a very short distance there is a big beautiful river of ice cold, clear water. Over the years, we saw numerous wild life, Mule Deer, Bear and Mountain Lions. The beauty of the Ponderosa Pine trees and deep blue sky is breathtaking.

I mentioned its people. All the years I worked meeting the public, there were very few who were inconsiderate or not friendly. No one can complain about the weather in Oregon. We don't have the terrible snow and cold as they do in the East or the hurricanes and tornadoes. We just have our rain to keep things green and from time to time a snowstorm or two. I often think to myself how fortunate I am to live in Oregon and that Mama and Dad had the courage to move here."

What milestones do you reflect on?

"Oh my, let's see:

– I've had a full life with my family
– Living on the farm in Buena Vista.
– The fire at our house and Dad being burned.
– The terrible time when we lived in La Grande.
– When Bert and I were married and the wonderful life we had together.
– The wonderful family Thanksgivings and Christmases.
– When the war was over.
– That awful day when Bert died.
– The loving concerns and care extended to me during that awful time.
– The passing of Mama, Dad and all my Brothers and Sisters. I'm the last one living.
– I am very fortunate to have wonderful nephews, their wives, and families, who are my 'kids'"

Authors note: *this poem was a favorite of my Aunt Babe and Uncle Bert:*

> *"God grant that I may fish until my dying day,*
> *And when it comes to my last call,*
> *I then most humbly pray,*
> *When in the Lord's landing net I'm peacefully asleep.*
> *That in His mercy I be judged*
> *As good enough to keep"*
> — Author unknown

EDGAR BOWEN

Born February 9, 1926
Coos Bay, Oregon

"what greater grief than loss
of ones native land."
— Euripides 484 BC

In writing this memoir of Oregonians, there are no better people to write about than Native Americans, who were born and raised in Oregon. At least seven generations have lived in our state and if it were not for them, the Lewis and Clark Expedition most likely would have perished. Numerous early pioneers owed their existence to the American Indian. Lest we forget, Native Americans taught the first Pilgrims how to survive. During a recent gathering of Native Americans from around Oregon, I was referred to Edgar Bowen who is a member of the Coos, Lower Umpqua and Siuslaw Indians. I met with him at their Tribal Hall in Coos Bay Oregon.

Coos Bay was originally named Marshfield when it was

45

founded in 1850 and its name was changed to Coos Bay in 1944. Coos Bay and the neighboring town of North Bend often referred to Coos Bay-North Bend, are located on the southwestern Oregon Coast where the Coos River enters Coos Bay, the largest bay in Oregon. In its 'heydays' Coos Bay-North Bend was the center for trade of coal, timber, lumber, and the fishing industries, most of which have vanished.

The story of the Confederated Tribes of the Coos, Lower Umpqua and Siuslaw is heartbreaking and I strongly recommend reading their history and information about their culture, villages, tools and utensils, clothing, religion and other pertinent information and view the outstanding video, 'Right the Wrong'.

When I arrived at the Tribal Hall, Edgar was in a meeting with the other Elders of the Tribes. Upon hearing that I was there, he immediately welcomed me and introduced me to his fellow leaders of the Tribes. As we sat in the small office of the Hall, his presence and bearing became evident to me why he was the Senior Chief of the Tribes. He instantly made me feel at ease as we talked for hours. Some of the most enjoyable hours I have ever spent.

After our visit, he proudly gave me a guided tour of the Tribal Hall and the Confederations, modern and large offices which house a Dental Clinic, Tribal Court, human resources, environmental and geological offices of the Tribes. When he introduced me to the many employees who serve Tribal members, I could see the respect and, yes, love they have for Edgar and why his Indian name is 'Tyee' (big). The respect they showed him is second to none that I have ever witnessed.

Edgar was recently honored when he was presented with the 2009 Lilah Bidwell Human Dignity Award by the Human Rights Advocates of Coos County, Oregon.

Edgar is five foot- eight and weighs two hundred plus. He has a full head of snow white, Collar-length hair. He has a happy and pleasant expression on his large face with the complexion

*of his heritage. Wearing stylish wire rim glasses that bring out
dark brown eyes which seem to twinkle in delight when he talks
about 'his people', he is an extremely proud man, proud of his
ancestors and heritage, and takes great pride in telling the story
of his Tribes.*

What is the history of your ancestors and family?

"For over ten thousand years, our Tribes have called the land
located along the central   Oregon Coast home. In 1908, President Theodore Roosevelt formally designated part of our ancestral
homeland as part of the Siuslaw National Forest. But our tribal
members don't need a formal designation to remind them why
this area is so special. It's a place where we can come and be
ourselves and be in touch with the earth—to be in the quiet of
the forest and sky. The forest is a spiritual place where we can
feel the connection and see the forest, smell the forest, and hear
the forest.

Protecting this land and preserving the cultural traditions
that surrounds it is a vision that is born of the terrible injustice
that happened over one hundred-fifty years ago. The Tribes
signed a Treaty in 1855, which set aside 1.6 million acres of our
land and promised things, including a reservation, educational
and economic help. For a variety of reasons, none of this came
to pass since Congress has never ratified the Treaty.

When the three Tribes (Coos, Lower Umpqua and Siuslaw)
signed the treaty, the tribal members were immediately and forc-
ibly removed from their land. Not by the United States
Government nor the U.S. Army, but by a militia of white home-
steading vigilantes. The vigilante–militia rounded up the Coos,
Lower Umpqua, Siuslaw and some Coquille Indians and marched
them on the "long walk' up the coast to the north spit of the
Umpqua River just north of where Reedsport is (approximately
27 miles).

They spent a winter on that barren land. All the male Indians
had to go. If Indian girls married vigilantes, they didn't have to

go, however, when the vigilante grew tired of her he just discarded her with the rest of the Tribe.

The next year during the winter, they were then marched up over the mountains along the coast of where Yachats, is located (approximately 34 miles). They spent two years there and were then marched to the Siletz Indian Reservation (east of Newport Oregon).

On the 'long walk' a totally blind Indian lady known as Amanda followed along good on the rocky and muddy trail until they started up over the high, rocky mountain where the Sea Lion Caves are now located. It was raining and the narrow trail was muddy and slick causing Amanda to fall. Finally the vigilante-militia got tired of her falling and holding up the line, they just picked her up and threw her over the cliff to the ocean below (over 200 feet). The vigilante-militia thought they solved their problem with Amanda, but after they got north of the mountain and back to the beach, there was Amanda sitting on the beach drying off. Being blind, she got a lot of respect from the militia. When the militia leader asked her how in the world did she ever swim there, she asked back, how did they know which way to go. She told them and I quote, 'I listened to the sound of the ocean surf hitting the cliffs and just swam around it.'

The Tribes had a hard time. They were not allowed to travel far to get food and supplies. They were told to plant wheat. Can you imagine wheat growing in our damp, wet climate here at the coast? To survive, they scrounged for food, dug clams, scraped muscles off the rocks in the cold ocean and ate whatever they could find. So the crops they were forced to grow so close to the ocean failed, and half of the Tribes perished due to starvation, disease and inhumane living conditions.

When the Tribes left the reservation and returned to their land and homes, they found that their old houses had been taken over by the whites. Indians lived where they could and some began to work as servants, fishermen and farm workers. As time went on, they married with non-Indians and some even became ashamed of their Indian origins because of the prejudice they faced.

Many never forgot the suffering of their ancestors and that a treaty had been signed, a treaty that had never been honored or ratified. The Coos, Lower Umpqua and Siuslaw have worked to pursue payment for land claims and are the longest continuous government south of the Columbia River.

Out of the thousands upon thousands of acres our Tribe once called home, we now only have 800 acres that are scattered around Coos and Lane counties. At the present time, there are 400 members of the Confederation of Coos, Lower Umpqua and Siuslaw Tribes left.

The Eisenhower Administration, in the 1950s, believed it was time to get rid of the 'Indian Problem' by simply declaring that our tribes did not exist and they stopped all government-to-government relations with us. This policy was called 'Termination'. In 1956 Congress passed a bill "terminating" all the tribes in western Oregon and the Klamath Tribe. Our Tribe vigorously opposed termination. Now a new Indian battle was on, the fight to reverse termination. Eventually the federal government changed its policies and disavowed termination. When the government got rid of us along with the other 64 Tribes in Oregon in one shot, they had a meeting at the Siletz Reservation and told us that we were now citizens of the United States. Can you imagine they let us be citizens?

The 7½ acres where this building, our Tribal Hall is, was donated to the Tribes in the 1920's and taken into trust by the Department of Interior for the Tribes forever because it was donated by a private party. When the U.S. Government terminated us, this land being in trust, and since it did not come straight from the Federal Government in trust for the Tribes, it came through the public community and free land that had been donated back to the Tribes, there was no way to get rid of it. So The Bureau of Indian Affairs had to go ahead to keep it in trust for us, even though we had been terminated as a Tribe. So, we already had this land in trust when we were reinstated in 1984. After termination, every month we would have a meeting here in the hall and reach in our pockets for money to pay the light bill and things. We maintained all these years until restoration.

One time we came up here to a Sunday meeting and saw a survey outfit working around our property. They had stakes all over the place and were busy as bees. We asked them what they were doing. They told us that the City of Coos Bay is selling the land to them and they were going to build a housing development. We immediately asked them what did they mean that the City is selling to them. They replied that since the Tribe had been terminated, the City's going to sell the land to them and that they were going to build houses on it. As you can see, it never happened.

Our Tribe was restored in 1984, and since restoration we have been working hard to improve the social and educational status of our people and recapture our history and heritage.

We purchased the land and the building where the offices, clinic and court sit from a local fraternal organization. We have spent over 2 million dollars remodeling it for our use with displays of our heritage and our people. To this day, our Tribes remain the only federally recognized Oregon Tribes that have not received compensation for taken lands. Nor have we had land restored by the United States Congress. We continue to petition Congress to correct this wrong.

What is the earliest recollection of your family life?

As far as my personal family goes, I don't know much about my Dad's side of the family other than that he was born and raised in Almo, Idaho down by the Utah border. His folks, my Grandparents Bowen, died very early and his older brothers and sisters took care of him. There were ten kids in the family. The Bowen name comes from 'bow-man', a man who shoots with bows. I never knew my grandparents Bowen. My Grandmother's name was Alice Laws-Bowen. I would guess that Grandfather Bowen worked in logging.

I can trace my mother's family to my Grandparents in around 1843, somewhere around there. My Grandfather Peter Jordan and two of his friends, a Talbot and an Ingersaw are still represented in their Tribe. Jim, you just met a Talbot when you came in.

He met my Grandmother, Louise Hilderbrandt when they were going to high school at the Chemawa Indian School in Salem, the oldest Indian School in America. At first he wanted to marry a Coos Indian girl he met there, but the Coos Tribe wouldn't let people marry within their own tribe. So later he fell in love with my Grandma who was a member of the Colville Indian Tribe in southeastern Washington. After high school they married and moved to this area. Descendants of them have been here ever since.

My Dad moved from Idaho and was a logger in the area. My Mother was born on September 18, 1898 and was one of fifteen children. She was a member of the Coos Tribe. They lived in the Tenmile area just south of Coos Bay and my dad worked as a logger. I was born here in Coos Bay in tough times. I have an older sister and a younger brother. We moved to Klamath Falls when I was a year old or so. When I was ten or so, I remember that I was very little, and sick, and in the hospital. They put me in a bed and Mother put a curtain over me to keep the flies off me. I remember it was Easter and they used to get milk in glass bottles and the milk man came in and gave me an egg, a colored egg, boy was that pretty. They gave me up for dead and sent me home. I don't know what I had.

We lived in Bonanza (just north of Klamath Falls). We called it 'snake ranch' were we lived. I had a saddle horse and I'd saddle it up and get on it and stay on it all day so I didn't have to get off it because of big rattlesnakes.

We lived in Klamath County until the sixth-grade. Dad worked in the sawmill as a green-chain 'puller'. When work got scarce, we moved back to Coos Bay in 1939 and lived with my Grandma Jordan and family for awhile. There were fifteen children in that family. It was tough, but somehow we got through it."

What do you remember about the weather?

"Over there in Klamath Falls it was extremely cold in the winters and hot and dusty in the summers. I remember there were flies everywhere. I was just a kid and in the summer the days seemed to last forever. The days were long and in those days you went to bed with the chickens. When it got dark, you went to bed, and when it got light, you got up. You stayed in most of the winter, and out most of the summer.

I remember one winter when we had an awful snowstorm and it blew big, deep drifts of snow and the men had to go out and shovel the drifts away from the houses and off the roofs.

The worst we ever had here was the Columbus Day Storm in '62. I lived in Dora, northeast of Coquille. It blew my garage down and a walnut tree fell on my roof. We were out of power for about a month.

Sure it rains a lot here. That's what keeps our forest green. Both summer and winter are mild. Did you notice the flowering cherry trees in bloom, and its only February. I'll bet they're not blooming in Salem. We've had rumors of tidal waves and big windstorms. Luckily they never happened."

What was school like?

"Well, I was in Klamath Falls when I started the first grade. My mother didn't send me for the first year 'cause I was immature. So I failed the first grade. The next year, mother assured me that I would love school, that my teacher would be young, that she would be beautiful and that I would enjoy school. So I goes to school and believe it or not, she was pretty, and she was nice, and I was starting to do pretty good until Columbus Day. The pretty and nice teacher told us that Columbus had discovered America. My mother never taught me that Columbus had discovered America. I thought, 'what is going on', and wondered what else they were lying about. It went downhill from there on. That year school started in September and in October, it stopped. I failed the first grade. I was getting bigger so they passed me to the second grade. I went to the third grade and they gave a test, a standard test, so I took the test and was the lowest in the whole class. They kept me in the third grade another year. So, two years in the first grade, and two years in the third grade. When I got to the fifth grade, we were living in Bonanza and it was so darn cold and we lived clear out in the boondocks. I had to catch the school bus. I hid behind a rock most of the time and went back home. So I wasn't much of a scholar.

I went to high school for a year in North Bend. They called it 'pony slough prison'. As I said, I wasn't much of a scholar so after one year I quit school and went to work at the shipyards in Vancouver, Washington. While I was in the Navy I figured that I'd better go back to high school and get an education if I wanted to make something of myself. When I got out, I went back to high school and graduated from 'pony slough prison' in 1948.

After high school I really didn't know what I wanted to do. I did know that I didn't want to be a logger or work in a sawmill. I thought about being a carpenter so I went to college to learn how at Oregon Technical School in Klamath Falls. That didn't work out so I went to Southern Oregon College in Ashland, graduated, and then to the University of Oregon where I got my secondary teaching degree."

When did you see your first car. When did you drive your first car. What kind of cars did you have?

"I guess the first car I ever saw was a Model T Ford my Dad had. He also had a great big old thing that had wood wheels on it. The fascinating thing about it was that it would out- run every dog in the neighborhood. I remember I'd get in the front seat and tell the neighbor kids that the thing would go seventy miles per hour. They said nothing goes seventy. I said 'oh yeah', and I just kicked the dashboard and the speedometer in the dash board just rolled around 'til it reached 70.

I saw hundreds of them, some most people have never heard of. There was Reo's, Terraplanes, Hudson's and Oldsmobiles. You know, you never saw as many cars as you see today though. I fooled around in my Dad's car in the yard at Bonanza before I started school. I think I was six. The Model T's had three pedals in them. One day I made it down the road about a mile and they had to come after me.

I got my first driver's license when I got out of the service. I was going to High School and the guy who ran the shop told me to take his car and go to town and get something for him. I told him that I didn't have a driver's license. He told me to take the car and go get myself one. That's how I got my first license. The first car I owned I think was a 1936 Plymouth. One of my buddies stole it and rolled it. I then had a DeSoto. It had electric wipers and when I got going fast I could pull a lever for over-drive."

Did you know anyone who served in World War I?

"Not really. My Dad was too young for the first war and too old for the second one. I was told that some of the men in our Tribes served."

How did prohibition affect your family?

"My mother's brothers had stills and made liquor. They'd take it in their big overcoats down the railroad tracks in Reedsport and sell it. They lived way out in the sticks about as far in the forest as you could get, so nobody bothered their stills.

When I got back here after the war, they used to have a green sticker about the size of a license plate that had three things on it; a drunk in a top hat leaning against a lamp post, a baby in diapers, and an Indian doing a war dance. That's the people they wouldn't serve liquor to. I think the poster was put out by the Oregon Liquor Commission."

How did the Great Depression affect your family?

"Well when I look back on it, I remember that we didn't have any milk or meat. We ate lots of vegetables and I haven't ate much vegetables since then. I'm quite a meat eater. Times were poor and we never knew we were poor, everybody was poor. Our neighbors were poorer than we were. Poverty has a smell about it. It really does. It wasn't good, there was no aid, no Social Security, nothing to back anybody. It was a shame that so many people went hungry in the land of plenty.

During the depression one of our neighbors had an old radio. The only way it would work (is) you had to stand and hang onto the antenna knob. My job would be to go over there every Friday night and hold onto the knob and listen to the fights with the men. Joe Lewis would knock somebody out every week. When I got older I figured I was just the ground for the radio, I didn't know that at the time. We listened to Joe Lewis and Henry Armstrong. Henry would fight anybody. My Father started a thing. Dad would send me around to collect dimes from everybody to bet on the fights. It cost them a dime and they picked out which round the fight would end and who would win the fight. Half of the pot went to the round winner and the other half went to the one who picked the winner. It was something to do and kept minds off their problems. Neighbors helped neighbors with a loaf of bread or a cup of sugar, anything to help to survive."

When did you meet your wife?

"I met my wife, Mary Anne Walker, in a psychology class in college in Ashland at Southern Oregon College. I was talking to the girl who was sitting next to me and she was sitting on the other side. Mary Anne kept butting in. Later we got to talking and dated during college.

We were married in 1955 at the Pioneer Methodist Church in Coquille, Oregon. I didn't invite anybody and she didn't invite anybody 'cause her father, he didn't think I was any good, and he didn't think it would be a lasting thing. He went around telling everybody what a bum I was. When he found out I was going to marry her, he finally came around on the last day and gave her away. We weren't expecting him to show up. Then he went around town and told everybody what a nice son-in-law he had, even better than his own son.

We were married forty-two years and had four kids. Our son passed away and our three daughters are all leaders and live here on the coast. Marry Anne passed away in 1997 and now I live with one of our daughters in Bandon. None of our kids got married, so we don't have any grandkids."

What do you remember about Pearl Harbor?

"I can remember the day it happened on a Sunday when I got news about eleven in the morning. My whole family went to see my sister who was working on a chicken ranch just east of Coos Bay. We had a heck of a time getting home. The vigilantes were at the end of the bridge with guns and stopping every car and going through everything. There was all kinds of rumors about the Japs landing on the beach. After school I spent four or five hours every night watching for airplanes in an old abandoned church and called in the type and direction they were flying.

A lot of the local men went down immediately and joined the National Guard. They thought that they would be able to stay here and guard the coast. They were sent down to Camp Robert's in California and then to the South Pacific to fight the Japs."

Did you serve in World War II?

"I signed up in the Navy when I was seventeen. I turned eighteen in boot camp in Idaho. After I got out of boot camp, they shipped us by rail to Treasure Island in San Francisco Bay and gave us four hours leave. The next morning they loaded us on a ship and we shipped out for the South Pacific.

I was put on another ship and we went to Guadalcanal and from there I went to a PT boat base to be on PT Boats. The reason they sent me to the PT Boat base was that they lost my records. When they finally found them, they shipped me back to Guadalcanal and transferred me to an LST as a gunner. The LST (Landing Ship Tank) was a 280 foot long, shallow draft ship that could carry around 2,000 tons. It was armed with 50 caliber machine guns and 40 millimeter anti- aircraft guns. I was a number one loader on one of the 40's and I didn't know what a 40 millimeter was. So they assigned me to that, and we were off to war.

The '40' had one guy who moved the gun from right to left and another guy moved it up and down. The guy who moved it from right to left also had a gun sight and shot the gun. They gave us target practice before we reached the Marshall Islands. There was a plane towing a sock about two miles behind. We opened up on it and some of the guns were shooting at the plane. Pretty soon, the pilot got mad, dropped the sock and just took off.

I remember being almost killed just about as many times by our own Navy as I was by the enemy. We fired those guns so much the barrels got so hot the grease just dripped out of it. I loaded the clips of 4 shells and was kept real busy during combat. From time to time, the gun would misfire and I'd have to get the bad shell out of the gun and throw it overboard.

We always had trouble when we landed due to the weight of the LST. When we landed on Okinawa we just landed with no trouble. We got all the tanks and stuff off and then an air-raid started. The Japanese planes would get low around our ships and our planes and we couldn't shoot at them. Our LST was on the beach with a slow slope up a hill. It wasn't very high and this American plane was chasing a Jap plane that started up over that hill. That was his mistake. He should've gone over our ships. He couldn't get away and started up and our plane shot him down. He went up over the hill and crashed right into one of our ammo dumps. It blew up for three days.

When we got back to Guadalcanal we were real good at shooting. We went to Saipan but didn't land and then back to the Marshall Islands and then to Guam. We hauled Marines and landed them on the islands.

When the War ended, we went from Guadalcanal to Yokohama, Japan. There was nothing left in Yokohama, there wasn't any Yokohama. The only building that was left was a big old hotel. It wasn't in too good of shape and the Army had taken it over for its headquarters. We didn't do much in Yokohama. We'd go to town every day and celebrate the end of the war. I was surprised the Japanese people treated us real good.

We gave our ship up to the Japanese to bring their troops home from China. They had almost two-million troops in China."

Did you experience any prejudice?
"Well the Blacks served the Officers. Once in a while they'd have a Philippine fella. They couldn't segregate us 'cause we were 'GI', but they didn't promote Indians. I went in as an Apprentice and came out a Seaman First Class. I was in there almost three years before I got my third stripe and everybody on-board ship had one, except me. There were quite a few Indians from Oklahoma and they weren't promoted either."

Where did you work?
"When I quit high school, I went to work building those little 'Jeep Carriers' for the Kaiser Shipyards in Vancouver, Washington. I lived in the company house, ate in the company café, bought things in the company store It got so noisy and I worked

crazy hours, I didn't like it, so I told them that I was leaving. They told me that I couldn't go. 'If you do', they said, 'we'll draft you in the Army'. We gotcha where we want you and you're not going anywhere. We need you right here. 'Well', I said, 'that's okay, catch me', and I took off.

When I went to get my pay, they docked me for everything. Evidently, I owed my soul to the company store. I was a go get 'er for tools and they charged me for everything I lost and most I didn't. By the time they took everything out from my pay, I barely had enough to get back to Coos Bay. When I got home I joined the Navy.

When I got home from the Navy I went back to High School and worked as a Longshoreman after school and in the summer.

I started teaching school in 1952 in Sitkum which is about half-way between Roseburg and Coos Bay. I taught five grades in a one-room schoolhouse. I remember I made a whole week of lesson plans. By ten o'clock on the first day , my lesson plans were all used up.

From Sitkum, I taught the Seventh Grade at the Sunny Hill School in Hause for two years. From there I taught at Dora, Oregon which is seven miles south of Sitkum. They kept closing the schools down and I moved from Dora and went to Arago. I taught there until they closed it down and moved to Myrtle Point. I taught at the Myrtle Crest Junior High School and retired in 1982.

Since I retired I do what I want, when I want to do it. Most of the time I work for the Tribes a lot and helped get back their restoration we have fought for, for thirty years, and work on Indian business which never ends."

What events do you recall in Oregon?

"In July, 1936, I was in Klamath Falls. My wife's family owned a cabin in Bandon. I heard on our radio that the whole town of Bandon burned clear down except that big building at the end of town. The cabin was also only one of four that was left. The fire got so big they couldn't control it. The fire started on a dry day when they were logging. They think when they ran a cable over a log, it caught fire and the west wind blew the fire into town. It was the second big fire Bandon had. Indian lore said there were three fires there, so I guess another one is coming."

What do you love about Oregon?

"What do I love about Oregon? Everything, I've been half-way around the world and I always come back. I like the climate, it's not too hot, not too cold. I'm permanent here and I think there's something to be said about permanence. If you are permanent, some way you'll make it even in the worse of times. If you're just moving around the country and it hits you hard, you probably won't make it. So I feel quite secure here.

I feel quite fortunate that my people love me and I have a lot of friends. I love my people, our ancestors and our heritage. My Grandfather was a Chief as well as was my mother. She was a great influence on me and a good teacher on how to get along with people and to treat others as you would want to be treated.

I love my work for my people. People always ask me how I got to be a Chief. Well, when I first became Chief, people just started calling me that, I thought its a nick- name or something. In those days you had to have a following, nobody elected you. If you had a following and a leader, you were Chief. I guess due to the influence my Mother had on me, I'm a leader, I don't know. The U.S. Government, since then, wanted to pattern our government here after theirs. They wanted everybody elected. When I was first became Chief or was conscious of it, I wasn't voted in. That's the way they did it."

What milestones do you reflect on?
– "When our Tribe was terminated and reinstated.
– That our Tribe is the only one that is not recognized by the United States Government.
– The many stories of our ancestors.
– Our ancestors signed a Treaty in good faith and to this day it has not been ratified by Congress.
– We have the copy of the Treaty given us when we signed it.
– The development of our building and offices of the Confederation.
– My wife, our wedding, marriage and her passing.
– Our children who are all leaders.
– The many kids I had the honor of teaching.
– That I am able to help my people."

Authors note: *the following is one of Edgar's favorite passages from the Bible:*

> *"Inasmuch as ye have done [it] unto one of the least of these my brethren, ye have done [it] unto me."*
> — St. Matthew 25:40

HELEN ETHELL

Born October 11, 1908
The Dalles, Oregon

*"The longer I live,
the more beautiful life becomes."*
— Frank Lloyd Wright

*I first met Helen on January 24, 2009. She lives with her
daughter Rose in a mobile home in a small town east of Salem.
Helen is 100 years old, a little hard of hearing, suffers macular
degeneration of the eyes and wears large glasses Her small hands
are gnarled with arthritis. Her mind is 'sharp as a tack', and her
memory, the history and life of her family and her sense of humor and wit are remarkable. Helen is four-foot ten inches and
weighs around ninety pounds. Her small face, somewhat wrinkled
with age and hard work, is accented by an ever-present smile
and snow-white hair.*

*Seven months earlier, she fell and broke her hip requiring
her to recuperate in a nursing home. Returning to her home, she*

walks with the aid of a walker, politely refusing her wheel-chair.

As we sat in the small living room of one of her daughter's mobile home, we were surrounded by numerous pictures of her large family which includes many great, great-grandchildren. I was utterly amazed at this lady. She made my wife and I welcome and feel at ease as she recalled her ancestors and her life in Oregon.

What is the history of your family?

"Oh my. My family goes way back especially my Great-Great Grandfather Kruger on my dad's side. My grandmother told me stories her mother told her why people left their homes and farms in Illinois and moved to Oregon. During the late 1830's and early 1840 they had bad floods that ruined their crops. There was a depression in 1837 and most of the banks went broke and people lost their money. My great-great grandfather Henry Harrison Luse with my great-great grandmother Elizabeth Vandervort-Luse lived in Illinois and in 1843 packed up their things in a covered wagon and set off on the Oregon trail for a better life. Many people lost their lives on the Oregon Trail, which was lined with graves of men, women and children. Great grandmother Elizabeth Vandervort-Luse was sixteen and she and her sister had to hide from the Indians as the Indians had never seen a white girl before.

The trip on the Oregon Trail was long and hard. The Oregon Trail ended south of The Dalles, Oregon. To get to Portland, they, along with other Pioneers, loaded their covered wagon on wooden rafts to get to Portland down the Columbia River, six months after they left St. Louis Missouri.

Great-great grandfather Henry Harrison Luse became big in timber and lumber, owning several saw-mills in the Santiam Canyon. Lumber in California was in big demand and he built a sawmill in Empire City near Coos Bay. They used oxen to get the large logs from the forest to the nearby mill. In order to get the lumber to California, he built large sea-going boats. His boats were so popular he started a boat yard and built boats and sold them to shipping companies all over Oregon and California. In 1900 he sold the saw-mills and the boatyard and moved to San Francisco where he retired very wealthy and had one of the largest private collections of first edition books and manuscripts. Losing everything in the 1906 earthquake and fire that destroyed the city, he died a pauper. Great Grandmother Luse lived for a short time in a boarding house where she died broken-hearted.

My great-great grandfather William Vandervort came to Oregon about the same time, but I don't know when. He secured a grant of 640 acres from the government in the Brush College area. He, along with my great grandmother Emily Vandervort, worked setting up a school for Indian children in Grand Ronde. Their daughter, my grandmother Rebecca Lulu Vanderfort, married my grandfather, Benjamin Woods.

My grandparents, Benjamin Woods and Rebecca Vandervort-Woods, lived in the Sellwood area of Portland with my mother Esther Florence Woods. Grandpa Woods was a fireman long before Portland had a fire department. He was one of the first firemen hired by Portland when it formed its first fire department. I don't know anything about Grandpa Wood's family. The papers about them were lost along the way. My maiden name, Kruger, goes all the way back to my Grandpa Ludwig Kruger and is quite a story.

My Grandfather Ludwig Wilelm Kruger was born in Prussia, April 24, 1833 to rich farmers. In March 1854 at the age of 20 he came to America on a visitor's permit. He celebrated his twenty-first birthday aboard ship, which was blown off course and took a longer time to cross the Atlantic than scheduled. Passengers were required to furnish part of their food and his food container was handled so roughly that some medicine in the container spilled on his food making it unfit to eat. Some sailors gave him food or he would have been half starved. He left home in Prussia March 25, 1854 and arrived in Bremen, Germany March 28. He then took a ship from Bremen April 1, and entered New York Harbor May 17 and set foot in America on May 18th. He did not return to Prussia when his visitor's permit was up so the German government put a fine on him, which his father paid.

Five years after landing in New York he moved to Indiana and then by wagon to Warren County, Iowa. It is believed that he met Anna Mariah Cooley in Indiana who moved with her parents to Iowa.

While in Warren County, Iowa, he married Anna Mariah Cooley in 1860. It is believed that they first met in Indiana. He worked on the many farms in the area and the Orilla coal mine that was located on the Cooley homestead.

At the age of twenty-two, Ludwig enlisted in I Company, 18th Iowa Infantry in 1862 and entered the Civil War. According to the papers we have, the troops suffered a scourge of measles and many died. Ludwig served with the Regiment who were in terrible combat and he spent time in the hospital at Ft. Smith Arkansas. He was discharged in 1865 His discharge paper was stolen and he never received another one. His friends, who he served with, helped him get his pension of $8.00 that was later raised to $14.00. Returning from the war, he farmed in Iowa, and during the cold winter months worked in the coal mine. Ludwig and Anna had 10 children while living in Iowa. Their first son, Albert, died at the age of 4 months. The couple had twins in 1860, one of whom, John, died when he was five. Their third child Margreth died when she was 9. The other children are Ameila, William, Joe and my dad, Edward.

Edward Kruger (Helen's father) came to The Dalles, Oregon by train on November 16, 1901 from Iowa. Ludwig and Anna soon followed them and the families homesteaded near Mosier, Oregon. It's located about fourteen miles from The Dalles on the banks of the Columbia River and is named after the man who founded it. The homesteads were not successful for farming since crops could not grow on the hills around Mosier and there was scarce water. Ludwig and Anna then moved to The

Dalles and lived there until their deaths. My Father, Edward Kruger, married Esther Florence Woods in Mosier on May 11, 1905 and had seven kids, all girls, Fannie, Mary, Opal, Violet, Hazel, Doris and me (Helen).

Dad worked on the railroad in Portland and then in The Dalles where I was born on October 11,1908. Mom told me that they lived in a small three-room house with me and my six sisters. When work became scarce, my family moved to Salem."

Authors Note: The Dalles, Oregon is located in Wasco County on the banks of the Columbia River. The name comes from the French word 'dalle' meaning either 'sluece' or flagstone' referring to the rocks carved by the Columbia River and the Celilo Falls and rapids now inundated by the Dalles Dam. Lewis and Clark camped in the area on October 25-27, 1805. The Dalles was the last stretch of the Oregon Trail. Early Pioneers either continued their trip to Portland on rafts or boats down the Columbia or over the rugged Barlow Trail. In 1864, a U.S. Mint was established here to mint gold coins from the gold from Canyon City, Oregon. When the gold ran out, the Mint was closed in 1870. Like its early years today, The Dalles has a major railroad yard that services trains from Portland to Chicago and is a commerce center between Portland and Pendleton.*
*Source: Wikipedia Encyclopedia

What is your earliest recollection of your family life?
"We were poor and I don't remember a time when we weren't. Just after I was born Mom, Dad and my sisters moved to Salem and lived in a house owned by great grandfather Vanderfort in the Brush College area. In 1918 Grandpa Vanderfort helped Dad buy a small bakery in the Sellwood area of Portland.

At first, for a short time, we lived with my Grandparents Woods until Dad and Grandpa Woods built a home above the bakery shop.Dad got 'TB' and couldn't be around flour so he sold the bakery and we moved to a house in the Lents part of

Portland. Dad worked for my Granddad Kruger roofing and in the shipyards during the war.

At Christmas time, Dad would get a tree and we would decorate it with homemade things and candles. To keep the candles straight dad had to use special holders for them. We always celebrated Christmas on Christmas morning. Dad would light the candles. Being poor we received very few gifts. We didn't have much, but our home was always filled with love. Most of the time we would have Christmas dinner with my grandmother and grandfather Woods and all of us received gifts of clothing.

We lived in a tent in the McClay area when we first came back to Salem. Being poor, when I was young, I worked in the fields picking beans and berries. Dad was able to scrape enough money to buy a home on Fisher Road in Salem. After the house burned down in 1939, I helped him build our new house.

When I graduated high school I worked for one year with my Dad shingling houses. The cedar shingles smelled good, but the splinters really hurt my hands and it was hard work. When one of my girlfriends got married she was able to get me a part-time job at the Vallatine Cleaners in Salem. When the owner of the cleaners took off, leaving us for ourselves, the owner of the building let us keep working. It finally was purchased and became Capitol City Laundry and then later the Rawlin's Dry Cleaners. I worked for over fifty years in the same building on Broadway Street. I did all kinds of work from running the big washers to the dry cleaning equipment. I was their seamstress for years and when I wasn't busy, I waited on the front counter and helped with the books."

What do you remember about the weather?

"The summers were always sunny and we'd have snow every winter. Living in Portland we could see the Willamette River flood each winter. People complain about our rain, but that's what makes Oregon green and pretty. When we lived in Sellwood, there were many big green Douglas Fir trees near our house. We enjoyed climbing them. I made it almost to the top once. If we would've got caught we would have got in trouble.

The hurricane we had in 1962 was real bad and blew down many trees. I would like to have been a roofer then as so many roofs were blown away. I have always liked the weather in Oregon. It's not too hot in the summer and not too cold in the winter."

What was school like?

"When we lived in the Brush College area of Salem, from the first to the fourth grade, I went to the Brush College School. It was a small two-room school with a bell and we took turns ringing it in the morning. I walked to school each day no matter the weather. When we lived in Sellwood, I went to school there in the fifth grade. When we moved back to Salem, I attended Salem High School which was located where Meier & Frank is now (Macy's downtown) and graduated in 1926. My younger sister was part of the first graduating class at the new high school located on Fourteenth Street. I really liked school and was good at arithmetic and good with numbers. I didn't have to study hard and received very good grades all through school.

I really wanted to go to college and be a doctor. Dad and Mother took me to Eugene to visit the University of Oregon. We found that we couldn't afford it. Disappointed, I started working at the cleaners."

When did you see your first car, drive one and what kind was it?

"My grandfathers always had cars and I don't remember when I first saw one or what kind it was. Dad was real strict about driving and I got my first driver's license when I was nineteen. The first car I remember Dad having was a Model T Ford. I was a 'tomboy' and helped Dad fixing it. We took the motor apart, repaired it and put it back together again. I like fixin' anything mechanical. Being poor, we didn't take many trips out of town and because most of the cars we had were used ones and broke down most of the time, I helped Dad fix them and keep them running."

How did World War I affect you and your family?

"I really don't know anyone who was in it. My dad and grand-fathers were too old. We read in the newspapers and heard on our small radio the news about it. We just couldn't believe the loss of life and the gassing of the men. It must've been awful. I was very young during it and can't remember much about it. I was told later that many men from Salem suffered real bad in the fighting with some being gassed."

How did Prohibition affect you and your family?

"None in my family drank so it didn't seem to bother us none. There was liquor all around and I don't think it stopped many people from drinking. They just tried to hide it. A couple of the laundry customers were arrested for making and selling liquor."

How did the great depression affect you and your family?

"Being very poor, it didn't bother us much. Living on Fisher Road, we had a cow and raised chickens and a large vegetable garden. What we didn't use ourselves, we sold it or gave it away to hungry people. From 1934 to the start of World War II, my husband, Gail, worked at the paper mill in Salem and had a good income. I had a job at the cleaners so we got by somehow but it was terrible for most people."

When and where did you meet your husband?

"When I was working at the laundry my best friend intro-duced to me to Gail Ethell in 1934. Later that year we were married. Because Gail's folks were very poor, they didn't want to go into a Church in their meager clothing so we had the wed-ding at my parent's house on Fourth and Hood Streets in Salem.

We had five kids and when I went into labor, Gail would have stomach pains. He called them "sympathy pains". In fact when our daughter Rose was born, Gail was in the Army at Fort Ord for boot training. Having stomach 'sympathy pains' he knew she was born."

What do you remember about Pearl Harbor?

"The first we heard of it was from our small radio. Most of us didn't know where Pearl Harbor was. Rumors of all kinds were everywhere. The Japs were landing at the beach and were going to bomb the West Coast. Most everyone I knew was scared. I know I was. We listened the next day, when President Roosevelt declared war on the Jap's. The news of the bombing was just awful with some of the sailors killed being from Oregon. We were told that evening to not drive at night and to pull our window shades to keep light from shining through. I remember how dark our neighborhood was that night.

A few of my customers at the laundry had kids going to Willamette University and were in Honolulu at the time with the Willamette University football team when the team played a game there."

Did anyone in your family serve in World War II?

"Yes, my husband Gail. Right after Pearl Harbor, Gail enlisted in the Army. He was told since he had four kids, he would be deferred from serving. He signed up anyway, telling them that "he had a lot to fight for". With my kids, and Mom and Dad we saw Gail off to war from the train station in Salem. He was stationed at Fort Ord for his boot training. As I mentioned, while he was there, he experienced "sympathy pains" and knew our baby, Rose was born. After boot camp, he was able to come home for two weeks and got to see his new baby girl. We made the best of the short time just talking and being a family. The day he left was sad for all of us. I held onto him and tried to hold back tears. The girls looked on with tears in their eyes, not knowing if they would ever see their dad again. He kissed all goodbye and then he was gone off to war.

His unit was part of the 24th Army Corps, which was made up of Marines and the 10th Army. He told me later that they shipped out from San Francisco on a troop ship for an unknown destination in the Pacific. On Easter Sunday, April 1, 1945 they were awakened by the sound of heavy naval gun fire. They assembled on deck of their ship, boarded landing crafts and headed ashore to the Jap held island of Okinawa.

That evening, Gail and three of his buddies had dug a 'fox hole' and were on guard duty when the Japs attacked. They fired back at the wave of Japanese and fended them off. As they settled back to rest, a Jap grenade landed in the 'fox hole' and killed his three friends. Gail was unhurt physically but suffered from the loss of his friends.

His unit found most of the Japs in big underground tunnels and bunkers on the high ground. It took over three weeks of slow and tough fighting to secure the island. Gail said the Marines captured the airfield and the mountains in about two weeks of fighting. Later when Gail returned home we read that over 32,000 Americans were wounded and 11,000 were killed, three of which were Gail's best buddies. The Japs loss was 118,000 killed during the last major battle of World War II.

During the war, I had to wait in line to get our rationing stamps. We saved everything we could to help win the war. To get by, me and my girls planted vegetable gardens each year. I remember every night we had to black out our windows. Many of my friends and customers at the laundry's husbands or sons were wounded and some killed. We were lucky when Gail came home in one piece.

After the war, he was stationed in the Philippines waiting to come home. Returning home, we again became a family and Gail resumed work at the paper mill. Many nights he would wake up in fright and have flashbacks of the loss of his friends. Over the years, I don't think he ever got over it."

What events in Oregon history do you recall?

"I remember Mount St. Helen's exploding. I was living in Keizer and we drove to the Gervais overpass over I-5 and watched it all day long.

When the Capitol Building burned down in April 1935, we were living on D Street near Parish Junior High School. I was pregnant with June at the time. When we heard the fire engines we looked out the window and saw the smoke. We didn't know what was burning so we ran all the way up to Center Street and saw that the Capitol building was on fire. While we were watching the fire, I looked around and saw my doctor walking up to me with a stern look on his face. He told me in no uncertain words that in my condition I shouldn't be there and to slowly walk home. I stayed 'cause I wanted to see history. The next couple of days I paid for not doing what he told me."

According to the 'Oregon Blue Book' the history of the Capitol started when settlers wanted a government of their own to protect their rights and to keep records of who claimed the land. They wanted protection from Indian Tribes who did not want them to settle and claim their land. In February 1843 the settlers began to hold meetings at Champoeg, a settlement about thirty miles north of Salem. Joe Meek, a mountain man, listened to the debate and then said that anyone in favor of forming a state government should stand in line behind him. Others who were against setting up a government formed another line. Fifty two men in favor of forming a government and fifty men were against it. George Abernathy was chosen as the first governor of Oregon and held meetings in Oregon City which became the first state capital of Oregon. In August 1848, President Polk allowed the Oregon County to become a territory and appointed Joseph Lane of Indiana to be Oregon Governor and it was Governor Lane who decided to meet in Salem.

The location of the Capitol of Oregon changed many times over the years. The territorial capital was in Oregon City and *was moved to Salem. The citizens of Oregon City, Corvallis and Eugene did not like this, as they wanted the capital in their own town. At one time the capital was located at Eola (just west of Salem) and another time in Buena Vista. Finally the Congress in Washington D.C. decided that Salem was to be the capital of the territory.**

On December 30, 1855 fire destroyed the newly completed State house. It wasn't until 1876 when a new building patterned after the U.S. Capitol Building was completed. It was destroyed by fire on April 25, 1935. Yet another new building was dedicated in October 1938. Its exterior is white marble and features a gold-plated pioneer standing facing west with an ax. The walls of the vast rotunda have oil painted murals depicting early history in Oregon. The Governor's office, Senate and House of Representative chambers are located in the beautiful building.**

"When the October 12, 1962 Columbus Day storm hit, I was at work at the Rawlin's Laundry when I looked out and I saw tree limbs and debris of all kind flying through the air. All of a sudden we heard a large crash. The owner ran outside and found that the large smoke stack of the laundry had been blown down. They shut down the boilers and we were out of business.

I was living with my parents on North 4th Street and it took me a long time to walk home. There was all kinds of things blocking the sidewalks. I saw some electrical wires laying on the ground and I walked way around them. When I got home, Dad was looking over the house. We didn't have any electricity and we had to cook on an old wood "Dutch oven" Dad used when he went deer hunting. I was out of work for about a week until they got the smokestack fixed and the boilers running.

Sources: * The Salem Story
*   ** Oregon Blue Book*

What do you love about Oregon?

Everything. The beauty of it, the weather, the people and being able to live close to my family. All of them.

What milestones do you reflect on?

"The things I remember most would be:
– The history of my extended family.
– Christmas time.
– Helping my dad fix cars and roofing houses.
– Working all those years at the Laundry and Dry Cleaners.
– Running to see the Capitol burn and my doctor being mad at me.
– The story of my husband's terrible times during the War.
– My family."

*"you can only perceive real beauty
in a person as they grow older."*
— Anouk Aimie

ED LAMBERT

Born June 2, 1921
Salem, Oregon

"other things may change,
but we start and end with family."
— author unknown

When I told Ed's daughter, Jeannie, about this book she suggested that I might want to include her father Ed's story. After
hearing a little of his life, I jumped at the chance to talk with Ed
and listen to the story of his life. When I arrived at their home in
Northeast Salem, both Ed and his wife, Alice of fifty-nine years,
greeted me at the door with warm and friendly smiles. He ea-
gerly shook my hand, and welcomed me into their neat and well
kept home. At first, Ed said that he hoped that he could remember things, because he has dementia and has trouble recalling
the past. Both Alice and daughter Jeannie reassured him that he
could and if needed, they would help. Ed said," well okay", and
"let's gets started." He motioned me to sit as he sat down in his

recliner. During our talk, his mind was sharp and very few times did his memory fail him. With the help of Alice and Jeannie he seemed to enjoy remembering the life and times of his family.

Ed stands erect with a trim, in-shape body. He is about five foot eight and weighs one hundred forty pounds. His somewhat receding snow-white hair accents his deep brown eyes. With a constant friendly smile on his small face with small jowls, he has the look of ease with his life and circumstances. His wrinkled hands of age were in constant motion as he recalled his younger days.

What is the history of your family?

"Yes, in 1910 Ernest Fuhrer, my mother's younger brother came to Salem from Switzerland when he was twenty. He found employment and was happy with the move. He then encouraged the rest of his family to come to America and Salem.

My Grandparents on my mother's side, Johann and Annalise Fuhrer and their children Marthe, Lydia, Jacob, Paul, and Walter came to America and Salem in 1911. My mother, Marie who was the oldest didn't come with them as she was expecting her second child.

My Father, James Lambert, was born in Chez-le-Bart, Switzerland in 1877, and my Mother, Marie (Fuhrer) Lambert was born in Moutier in 1883. They were married in Switzerland and lived in Cudrefin, Switzerland until they came to America. In August 1912 they left Switzerland for America with my two brothers, Andre, five months old and John, two years old. On August 12, 1912 they took the steamship, *Chicago*, from Harve, France and arrived in New York City on September 17, 1912.

Mama told me when I got older about the trip from Switzerland on the *Chicago*. It was a fairly new ship that was built in 1908 and held 1608 passengers. To save money, they originally purchased second class tickets, but before they departed, a good friend recommended that they should up-grade their accommodations as the ones they purchased were very bad living conditions for the long trip. Mother said that she was so glad that they did as she was sea-sick the whole trip. They were also fortunate in that there were only 486 passengers on their trip. Taking over a month to reach America, it seemed like they would never reach their destination. Especially keeping track of a two year active boy and a five month old baby when she was so sick.

When they arrived in the New York City harbor all of the passengers stood on the deck and looked at the sight of the Statute of Liberty and the skyline of the city. When they were disembarking the ship, they couldn't find John, the two- year old. Frantically, they looked everywhere where a youngster could hide, finally finding him hiding near one of the life-boats.

After they were processed in at Ellis Island, they took the train from New York City to Portland and then on to Salem.

I don't remember hearing anything about any of my grandparents or great grandparents Lambert other than they all lived in Switzerland. All I can tell you about them is that the women really liked children and wrote to us all the time and sent us Swiss chocolates. They never forgot us. Those were the real Swiss chocolates."

What is your earliest recollection of your family life?

"Well, my dad was a person who worked as a horticulturist and was quite talented in that. When he first arrived in Salem, he was employed by A.N. Bush, one of the richest men in Salem. He worked for him until his death taking care of the fruit, walnut, and prune trees on the property located on Capital Street between Center and Chemeketa Streets.

I was born June 2, 1921 in the family home located on North 14th Street in Salem. I lived there with my two brothers John and Andre and my sister Antoinette until I joined the Air Corps. Antoinette was born in Salem in 1916 and was the brains of our family and a school teacher. As you can see, except for when I was gone in the Air Corps or when we lived in Florida, I haven't moved very far from my roots.

79

Well, I'd say anytime from when I was five or six years old, I had a pretty nice life. We didn't have a great amount of money, but we always had plenty to eat. We had a big piece of property there and my dad could make anything in the world grow. We had a huge lot and had all kinds of things growing there with several trees and walnut trees. We also raised chickens, so we had eggs and chicken every Sunday. My boyhood life was a pretty good life. We were never short on food as we had so much stuff growing. My dad built a green house so we had all kinds of things growing all the time. All we had to buy was our meat and milk, but not too much of that.

My dad died in 1929 when he was fifty-one years old. I was just seven years old. I remember he was lying on his couch in the living room when he died and a couple of things happened that were not too pleasant. I remember a man came by when Dad was on his death bed and asked my dad if he was afraid of dying. That was the stupidest thing I ever heard of. My dad just said, "no."

Us kids worked picking strawberries and beans in the summer to help Mama make ends meet and I worked as box boy for the Fred Meyer store in downtown Salem. I know it was real hard on my Mother with Dad dying. I know it was hard on me. I couldn't understand why. Mother died August 31, 1977 at the age of ninety three. My brother John worked with the telegraph and telephone company in Salem and died on March 25, 1985. Brother Andre also worked for the telegraph company and died in November 2001. My sister Antoinette who was a teacher died in November 1999."

What do you remember about the weather?

"Well, I don't know, there was quite a bit of rain and as a kid always looking for snow and hoping we'd have it. Otherwise the weather was good. We had plenty of good weather for playing ball out in the street and that sort of thing. When I was in the Air

80

Corps, my mom wrote me about a flood in January 1943 when the Willamette River flooded and washed the Mellow Moon Skating Rink in West Salem off its foundation and up against the Center Street Bridge. I remember the winters of 1950 and 1951 were very cold with snow, freezing rain and fog for a long time on end.

During the Columbus Day hurricane I was working at the airport and was able to get home. Our kids got out of school and went to the grandma's house on Nebraska Street for safety. We didn't have much damage to our house and only a couple of trees were blown down and some broken windows in the greenhouse. For two or three days we didn't have any power. Alice was working for a doctor downtown. During the height of the storm they made her take a patient home to south Salem before she could come home. She had to drive way out of her way. On the way to our house, a tree fell down right in front of the car. She had to abandon the car and leave it and ran about five blocks to grandma's house. Until the dams were built in the 1950's on the North and South Santiam Rivers we always had bad floods.

Well, the 1964 Christmas flood was called the worst disaster ever to hit the state by the Governor. So, for about a week we had real cold temperatures and deep snow and then we had a 'Chinook' (warm wind and record heavy, warm rain). The snow melted fast with the rain and started runoff in the Cascades and the Valley causing the Willamette and all the creeks to flood.

Many homes were flooded in the Keizer area with a lot of people having to be evacuated from their houses. Pringle Creek overflowed the dikes around the Salem Memorial Hospital and the National Guard had to evacuate many patients. I was working for United at the airport and a small plane crashed just south of the airport killing three men who had gone up to see the flooding. It was reported that if the dams on the Santiam Rivers would not have been there, the Willamette River would have crested at 37½ feet instead of 30 feet."

What was school like?

"I started school in the First Grade at Englewood School here in town. I was somewhat terrified. Well, I'm in the first grade and my teacher was Mrs. Grant. She was the most lovely woman I knew besides my own mother and Alice. So, Mrs. Grant was being substituted one day for one reason or another, I still don't know the reason. I went in the classroom and there was no Mrs. Grant, so I said to myself that I'm not going to stay here so, I was only six years in the first grade and I came out of there and they stopped me and took me up to the principal's office and held me there and wouldn't let me go home. I told them that I'm not going to school unless Mrs. Grant is here. I don't know how I convinced them, but they let me go home, six years old, to go home and I walked home by myself about six blocks away. When I got home, Mama brought me back. They had another teacher there and things were better and I stayed, but at first, if Mrs. Grant wasn't there, I didn't stay.

Mrs. Grant and I were great friends. When I worked at United Air Lines and every time Mrs. Grant came to fly with us, she'd come in the door and yell, 'Eddie.' We would banter back and forth and Mrs. Grant and I carried on like that for years. She was a wonderful woman.

I went through the sixth grade at Englewood and then to Parrish Junior High School. My first year I went to Salem High School when it was located downtown.

My junior year was the first class at the new high school on 14th Street. I didn't participate in sports. I was too puny. I would guess I was an average student and graduated the next year.

My friend, Charlie, was always getting me in trouble. He was a brilliant guy and we'd be sitting together and there'd be so much going on and finally the teacher kept separating us. Charlie would study for a few minutes and get an A. Sitting next to him, I struggled until they moved me far enough away for me to get a C. Charlie was great in his studies but seemed to get him and me in trouble. The next year, I attended Willamette University for one year and I went into the Army Air Corps.

English was not spoken at home during my growing up years, only German. My brothers and sisters had to learn English at school and in the community. My family are very proud of our education"

When did you see your first car? What kind of car was it?
"I got my first driver's license on my birthday. I was fifteen years old and I walked to the Capitol Building, took the test, took the car out and got my license. The first car I saw was a model A that my dad had. My first car was a 1932 Ford. We had never got away from Fords for awhile. The first car Alice and I bought was a 1949 Studebaker. It was no great thing for speed but was reliable. The reason I bought it is that my sister and her husband bought it and didn't have it for a month before they decided that and didn't want it, so they sold it to us for a very good price. After that I bought my cars from friends in the car business. I don't drive anymore, neither does Alice. Our kids won't let us. It's for our safety and others. However, I do miss it and sometimes I go out in the garage and just sit in my car and reminisce."

How did World War I affect you and your family?
"The only guy I know who served in World War I was my Uncle, Jake. He was a Swiss boy. He came over from Switzerland and as a matter of fact, he was not yet a citizen and was the first guy to go down and volunteer to get in the Army. Later on he never discussed his experiences in the war at all. I know that the family was very proud of him as his parents had just emigrated to America. He went on to be a Vice President at the Ladd and Bush Bank here in Salem."

How did Prohibition affect your family?

"Well, my grandfather always made a little wine for himself and whoever came to the house. I don't think he worried about it. He always made his own to the day he died."

How did the Great Depression affect you and your family?

"We lived and existed on the property we had. We didn't have any extra money and we didn't live a sort of life where we bought fancy clothes. We ate well. Mother made our clothes and did a lot of canning of fruits and vegetables.

When my dad died, Mother went to work for A.N. Bush at this home on Capitol Street. Mr. Bush gave my mother a job working in his laundry. He had a laundry in his big home as his wife was an invalid. He already had two ladies working in the laundry and with my mother he had three. They had to have fresh linens all the time.

Everybody I knew was poor. I remember that Mother never turned away hungry people. Our house was just a block away from the railroad tracks and many people would come by hungry. Mom would always have something for them. We had a large area in the back yard and had a couple of tables and some chairs for them to sit to eat as Mother would never let them into the house. Like I said earlier, all of us kids worked in the fields in the summer and worked many odd jobs to help out."

When and where did you meet Alice?

"In the summer of 1947, Alice came out to the Salem airport and bought a ticket on United Airlines to go back home in Ohio in a couple of weeks. I kept calling her up about her tickets at her home and at the Salem General Hospital where she worked. When she returned from Ohio, I asked her for a date. Well, that was the best thing that ever happened to me. We dated for about a year or so and were married on October 22, 1949 at the Center Lutheran Church on Capital Street. We had a small wedding and we flew on United to San Francisco. We both had brand new shoes and we got terrible blisters walking up and down the hills in San Francisco. That was kind of a miserable experience. We only had a three day honeymoon as we had to get back to work.

Our family includes our daughter Jeannie, born in 1954, sons Walter (Wally) born in 1957 and James born in 1953 and died in infancy."

What do you remember about Pearl Harbor?

"Well, I was in the Army Air Corps and stationed in Miami, Florida at that time. I think it came over the radio around 1pm our time. Where I was stationed there were only a few people there and it was a restricted area. When we heard the news it was really a shock and it was automatic practically that we were put on full alert. We all listened to the radio about the sneak attack and President Roosevelt's speech the next day. We were on constant alert for a long time."

Did you serve in World War II?

"That's the funny part of me trying to volunteer in the Air Corps. When I tried, they told me that I was already in the draft age and they turned me down every place I went. So, I was trying to find something where I'd be happy, so finally I was drafted in the Army and I hadn't been drafted more than a few days, they called me in and told me that I was put right into the Air Corps, exactly what I was trying to volunteer for.

The Army Air Corps was part of the Army and it wasn't until 1947 when it became the Unites State Air Force. My job was to keep track of airplanes where they were going and to plot flights.

I served different places all over, mostly in Miami, Florida and Watson Lake, Yukon Territory, Canada. One day I was in the heat and humidity of Miami and the next thing I knew I was in the freezing cold of Watson Lake in the Yukon. The outfit I was in was the 122nd Army Airways Communication System. The airfield at Watson was a link in the Northwest Staging Route

Program. Watson Lake is located in the Northern Rockies, near the Liard River and the British Columbia border. The Alcan Highway was nearby with all kinds of Army trucks hauling stuff to Alaska. It was really, really cold. You know, during one cold snap the temperature dropped to seventy degrees below zero. Boy was it cold. I didn't like cold then and I still don't. All kinds of airplanes flew in and out of Watson Lake, B-17, B-26 and fighters. I was a 'buck' Sergeant when I got out right after the War was over and came home to Salem. My brother-in-law was a gunner in the Air Corps and became an instructor for a while."

Where did you work?
"Well, I worked with my Brother. We delivered groceries for the Fred Meyer store that was located in downtown Salem on Liberty Street. I worked odd jobs during High School and in the fields picking the crops during the summer. I always had money coming in as I had some sort of a little job. When Dad died, I took care of my mother as my brothers were grown men and I drove her places and took her to work.

When I got out of the Air Corps, United Airlines was looking for help and was advertising for workers. United was starting to expand here so I went out to apply for a job. It was very simple, when the guy found out that I was in the Army Air Corps, he said, 'Okay that's good enough', and hired me right then and there. My job was taking care of customers, selling tickets, we did everything. At first we had D-3 airplanes. Everybody who worked there did everything. We never had any emergencies or accidents. We did have a couple of problem passengers though.

Working for United Airlines I was interested in flying and I can tell you a little bit about the Salem Airport and airplanes in Salem. The first airplane the people of Salem ever saw was a Curtis model airplane in 1910. It took off from the Lone Oak racetrack at the State Fairgrounds. From the accounts I heard, it circled around the Capitol dome.

The Salem Airport was dedicated in August 1929. It wasn't until 1941 before direct mail came to Salem on an airplane. In the spring of 1942 the U.S. Air Corps took over the airport and fighter squadrons came there to train.

In 1948 President Harry Truman flew into the Salem Airport as did President Kennedy in 1960. The first jet to fly into Salem was an F-80 in August 1948. Boy was that thing loud and fast. When United closed its operation in Salem in November 1979, I transferred to West Palm Beach, Florida. Working in Florida was a picnic compared to Salem, where I really worked! We had very few people and had a lot of different things to do, but in Florida, well all those guys were gold bricks, they tried to find ways to get out of work. I liked to work. I really liked West Palm Beach. That was a great job. When I retired from United in 1984, after forty years, we moved back here to Salem."

What do you love about Oregon?

"Well, let's see. I love the fact that all our kids stayed in Oregon and live nearby. We get to see them quite often. In fact every Thursday we get together here in our house. At first it started with our son Wally dropping in and then Jeannie and her husband Terry joined us. When Wally's wife passed on, I think our get together helped him with his loss. Later Wally's son Mike joined us. We have great times of hearing what's going on in our kid's lives. Lately, they take care of us, sorting and arranging our pills, taking care of the house and helping Alice with the cooking. I don't know what we'd do without their help and, yes, love. I haven't been to many places around America or the world, but I can't imagine a better place to live. Our winters are warm, sometimes wet, with very little snow and cold. As you've heard, my roots are here in Salem. I saw it grow into a beautiful city. All in all, I love living here."

What milestones do you reflect on?

– "Well, the stories my mother told me about the trip from
Switzerland to Salem.

– My memories of my first grade teacher, Mrs. Grant, and me
going home when she wasn't there.

– The hurricane in 1962 and the bad flood in 1964.

– The awful day when my dad died and the unpleasant things.

– Working with my brother in the grocery store as box boys.

– Me trying to enlist in the Air Corps and they wouldn't let me
'cause I was in the 'draft' and after I was drafted they
put me in the Air Corps, right where I wanted in the
first place.

– My time in the Air Corps. I enjoyed being in Florida, but not
the cold, windy and snowy Air base at Watson Lake.

– Getting my job with United Air Lines. I really liked the
work, especially when I first saw Alice coming into the
terminal. I couldn't take my eyes off her. Before she got
to the ticket counter, I arranged so that I could wait on
her.

– Talk about a 'milestone'; come this October 22nd we will be
married sixty years, can you imagine, sixty years
together. Like I've said many times, Alice is the best
thing that ever happened to me.

– Of course, the births of our daughter Jeannie, sons Wally
and James and when James died.

– Having our kids living in Oregon and visiting us every
Thursday.

– It doesn't get much better than this."

*"happiness isn't something you experience,
it's something you remember"*
— Oscar Levant

ELIZABETH " BETTY" ROTH

Born January 19, 1923
Oregon City, Oregon

*"Memories are the fondest things
we as humans have"*
— author unknown

*During a crab feed at a fraternal organization in Silverton
Oregon, Betty's son, Don referred her to me. When I first talked
with her that evening I was immediately impressed with her wit,
humor and wonderful outlook on life. Silverton, Oregon is located 12 miles east of Salem on Highway 213. It's the gateway
to the Silver Falls State Park, the largest in Oregon. It is also the
home of the Oregon Garden, an 80 acre botanical park.*

*Living by herself in her small, meager home since 1984, she
is surrounded by memoirs and pictures of her extended family.
To my wonderment, she is a "history buff" with boxes of docu-
ments, scrapbooks and pictures of her ancestors and family. I
was absolutely amazed at her memory, especially when she re-*

membered the exact day she graduated from High School. Her recollection of the stories of how one of Oregon's Governor's was killed and stories her father told her of a large forest fire. She's amazing!

Betty is five foot-one in her stocking feet and I would guess weighs one hundred-twenty pounds. On our first visit with her, she had just returned from having her short, somewhat gray hair washed and set in large curls and swept back. Welcoming us, she immediately made us feel at ease and welcomed by her outgoing, friendly and gracious personality. Her small round face, accented by designer glasses, and her small, twinkling eyes give off a look of complete and happy satisfaction with her life and surroundings.

At first I was somewhat confused about her first name. She explained that her mother always wanted a daughter named Elizabeth but her nickname Betty, short for Elizabeth was what everyone called her. As we talked for over three hours, listening to the story of her life and family and going through the boxes of history of her family, the time just seemed to fly by. She mentioned in passing that she fell breaking her ankle when she was walking on her wooden backyard deck. At first, she didn't know it was broken. She crawled on her hands and knees into the house and got her purse and car keys. Suffering from pain she had difficulty getting down the front steps and walking to her nearby car. Driving herself to the hospital she found all the emergency room parking spaces taken, "so I had to park quite a ways from the hospital and walk up a steep hill to the emergency room. The emergency room nurse took one look at it and told Betty her ankle was broken. The nurse helped her into a wheel chair and wheeled Betty to her doctor's office, which was located, down the hill from the hospital about a block away.

What is the history of your family?

"We have traced my Father Thomas' family back to 1687 and my Mother's family, Sprague back to 1606 in London England and they landed in Plymouth Mass. in 1623.

My great-great grandfather Lauren Lewis Thomas was born in 1817 and died in Silverton in 1883. He and his wife, Eliza Dimick-Thomas, left Rockford Illinois in 1846 and went to Independence Missouri where they secured a covered wagon and supplies for the long trip to Oregon. They arrived in Oregon on September 5, 1847 and built their cabin on a 640 acre Donation Land Claim in October 1847. The land was south of Pine Tree Four Corners near Butte Creek. The old Territory Road which is now Highway 213 northeast of Silverton and just west of the Scotts Mills, crossed great, great grandpa's land and extended from Oregon City ending at the Spores Ferry on the McKenzie River near Eugene. Great, great grandpa Thomas and his partner were hired by Thomas McKay to build a gristmill, a small sawmill and two cabins at the falls of Butte Creek during the winter of 1847-1848 where Scotts Mills is now. The small town of Scotts Mills is located on Highway 213, 19 miles east of Salem on the banks of Butte Creek.

The children of great-great grandma and grandpa Thomas included my great grandfather Lewis Lauren Thomas and the first triplets born in Oregon on August 12, 1850, Mariah, Alvin and Mary Thomas.

Great-great grandpa Thomas donated land and established the Thomas School District 67 in March 1866. The school was built in 1866 and was on a knoll just south of Pine Tree Four Corners. The Thomas School burned in January 1947 and the school district was merged with the Glad Tidings and Marquam school districts.

My Great grandpa Lewis Lauren Thomas was born in 1845 in Illinois and came to Oregon when he was two years in a covered wagon on the Oregon Trail. He passed away in 1877 and is buried in the Thomas family plot in the Miller Cemetery.

He enlisted in the Oregon Infantry Volunteers during the Civil War and was discharged in October 1865. He married Mehalia Hook-Thomas in 1866. Mehalia was born September 4, 1848 and came to Oregon with her parents John and Elizabeth Hook in 1864. Great grandpa and Mother Thomas had three children, John Thomas, George Thomas and my grandpa Emory Lewis Thomas.

My grandpa, Emory Lewis Thomas was born in 1873 in Monitor, Oregon. He married Jeanette Helena Mazingo who was born September 1879. They had four kids, one of which was my dad, Donald William Thomas. Like his ancestors, he worked in the woods logging and in sawmills in the area.

My dad, Donald, was born September 30, 1902 in Scotts Mills and passed away September 9, 1990. In 1922 he married Irene Violet Muff who was born October 11, 1905. and passed away March 8, 1984. They had five children, my brothers Albert, Donald Jr., my Sisters, Anna, Donna and me.

We could not trace the Mazingo family back very far. During the Civil War, to keep from having to fight in the War, men could "purchase" other men to take their place. The men taking the place would use the name of those they replaced. Evidently great-great grandpa Mazingo "sold" himself to take the place of a man named Mazingo and assumed his last name. He enlisted in the Army in Illinois and was shot in the hand and had small pox. When he entered the hospital, they burned all of his clothes and shoes. When he finally got out of the hospital they just gave him clothing and no shoes. He raised cain and wrote letters to the "higher ups" until they gave him a pair of well-worn shoes. Once a month, he rode his mule to get his Army pension of two dollars.

He was born in 1842 in Missouri and died in 1927. He married Mary Elizabeth Inman who was born in 1844. They had six children, Henry, Andrew, Ida Bell, Kate Ann, Jennaette Helena and Eliza Jane.

Both the Mazingo and Inman families braved the Oregon Trail. I was told that the kids had to walk all the way across the plains and that the hardships were terrible and many died on the trail. Great Grandma Mazingo was blinded in one eye by a dust storm during the trip. All of my family on my Dad and Mother's side goes way back in the history of Oregon. They made a living logging in saw mills and farming."

What is the earliest recollection of your family life?

"When I was born my family lived in Oregon City and my Dad worked at the paper mill. Just after I was born in 1923, we moved from Oregon City to Silverton. Dad worked in the woods logging and in the Silver Falls Saw Mill. We were poor but we never went hungry. Mother made most all of our clothes. When we got older, us kids worked picking strawberries and beans in the summer to help make ends meet.

Christmas time things were meager. Dad and my brothers cut down Christmas trees each year that grew in the Silverton hills. Church was, and is, an important part of our family life."

What do you remember about the weather?

"Most winters when I as a kid, it snowed. I didn't like snow and cold and I still don't. I think we had more snow then than we've had lately. I liked the rain and the windy storms we had. Living in Silverton, I don't recall any damaging floods. I do know the Willamette River would flood each year and that they had a bad flood at Vanport just after the War. My favorite time of the year was the Fall, the Indian Summers with warm days and cool nights. I loved to run and roll in the stacks of maple and oak leaves. In those days, we could burn the leaves and I loved the smell of them burning.

The Columbus Day storm in 1962 was awful. We lived on our farm just south of Silverton. We didn't have power for over five days. The electricity was out and the water pump couldn't run. Without water and lights, it was difficult, especially with five kids. The hurricane knocked down part of the barn and the sheep shed, and blew the roof off the chicken brooder house. Our neighbors suffered worse off than us when a large Douglas Fir tree broke off about half way up and fell right in the middle of their house. We are blessed living in Oregon with the mild climate. Sure we have rain, but not the damaging snow, hurricanes and tornadoes the rest of the country has.

I don't know if this is classified as weather but I will never forget when Mt. St. Helens blew up on May 18, 1980. I was in Seattle with one of my daughters and we were on our way to back to Silverton. When we got to Olympia, the State Police had shut down I-5 and were directing all the cars to the Olympia Brewing parking lots. Later that morning they let us leave and head for home. The freeway was crowded with cars and trucks and we could see the huge black cloud that rose. I was riding in the back seat of the car and was taking pictures of it. Just before we reached the bridge over the Tuttle River, I shouted to my daughter to speed up, the bridge may wash out. She shouted back to me that I had scared her to death as she sped up. We made it across the bridge but I remember seeing the river raging, full of trees, parts of houses and boiling mud.

When I got home I turned on the TV and watched the mountain destroy itself. There was pictures of the big ash cloud that rose thousands of feet in the air. It was reported that the I-5 freeway was closed for fear that the bridge we had driven across earlier would be washed out from the raging river. The TV reported that a huge bulge on the north side of the mountain gave way when an earthquake caused the north part of the mountain to slide away causing a huge landslide.

The next day pictures on the TV showed the huge mudflows that tore down the mountain into rivers destroying everything in sight. When the mudflow hit a logging camp, dump trucks big tractors and loaders and a huge 'cold deck' were tossed around like toys.

Later, pictures of Yakima, Washington were shown on the TV of the ash cloud blocking out the afternoon sun.

A couple of day's later, the TV showed thousands of acres of Douglas Fir trees blown down laying in the direction of the blast. It looked like someone had neatly laid them out in the same direction. It was reported that 57 people were killed along and numerous deer, elk and bear.

The first time it erupted we didn't get any ash or fallout in Silverton from it, but the second time it erupted we had a minor coating of volcanic ash covering everything,

You know, in the winter when St. Helens was covered with snow and the pink hue of the sunset, it looked just like a giant strawberry ice cream cone. Now our beautiful ice cream cone was half gone."

What was school like? Where did you go to school? Did you graduate high school or attend college?

"I started the first grade on January 1, 1929 in Silverton. In those days kids started school in January or September depending on their birth date. My first grade teacher was Miss Hubbs. When we moved to California I spent half of the sixth grade there. In 1936 we moved to Portland and I attended Washington High School and graduated on June 6, 1940. Because of the depression and very little money, none of us kids went on to college. I enjoyed school but most of the time the teachers were very strict. Both Mom and Dad made us study and get a good education."

When did you see your first car? When did you first drive one? What kind of cars did you have.?

"I don't remember when I saw my first car. It had to be around town here. Dad's first car was a 1929 Ford Model T. On the farm we had all kinds of tractors and trucks. I didn't have a driver's license but I drove all over the farm, especially during harvest. After Al died, I got my first driver's license in 1960.

Just the other day on my birthday, I renewed my drivers license for another eight years and my 1999 Chevy Lumina gets me where I want to go."

How did World War I affect you and your family?
"All I know about it is what I've read and studied. My Uncle John Thomas served in the Army in France."

How did Prohibition affect your family?
"I was only ten or so when it was over and I don't know much about it. To help keep food on the table, Grandma Thomas told me that Grandpa Thomas made home brew and my Dad sold it. I think I heard Grandpa Thomas also had a still in the hills above Scotts Mills."

How did the Great Depression affect you and your family?
"We lived in Silverton at the time and were really poor. We were never without food, but our meals were meager. Dad hunted deer and other wild game and each summer mother canned over five hundred Mason quart jars with fruit and vegetables. Dad worked in the Silverton Mill, and made $4.80 for a twelve-hour day loading box cars with lumber. One night when he got home from work he couldn't find his wallet. After dinner he returned to the Mill and completely unloaded the box car, found his missing wallet and reloaded the box car.

Mom always made clothing for us and shirts for the boys. Wearing 'hand-me-downs' like the other kids, we got by. Even when I worked in the shipyards, I wore dresses that Mom made for me"

When and where did you meet your spouse?
"I meet Alvin Roth (Al), my second husband in 1947. Howard Meyer a mutual friend of Al and me introduced us. At the time I was alone with two children. We courted for a couple of years

and were married January 3rd, 1949. Al adopted both kids from my first marriage and was really their father."

What do you remember about Pearl Harbor?
"At the time I was living in Portland with my friend Senora Woods. We were sleeping in when her mother knocked on our bedroom door and told us that the Japanese had bombed Pearl Harbor, Hawaii. We didn't know for sure where it was. We got up and listened to the news on the radio and read about it the next day and listened to President Roosevelt's speech. We were just eighteen and we knew right away that many of the boys we knew in school would be going off to war."

World War II, how did it affect you and your family? Did anyone in your family serve in World War II?
"At the time, I was living with my friend, Senora and working at the Newberry store in Portland. When the shipyards opened in Vancouver Washington, I got a job as a mimeograph operator. Like all others, we had blackouts and had to keep our windows shaded and couldn't drive at night. We saved tin cans, grease, paper and cardboard to help with the war effort. I purchased War Bond stamps and bonds when I could.

My Brother Al served in the Navy on a submarine. He told me that on the first "shake-down cruise" in the North Atlantic he stood watch with a bucket nearby because he was sea sick.

My husband Al, was a Seabee in the Navy and served in the Aleutian Islands in Alaska. He drove a big dump truck on one job, building an airstrip. He said that a mountain they called 'Bally Whoo Mountain' on the construction site was so steep the dump trucks couldn't make it up. They kept slipping back due to the heavy load. They finally had to use big tractors to push or pull the trucks up the hill.

Al also worked on the airfields on Saipan and the other islands in the South Pacific during the war. He told us that the

Seabees had to fight the Japanese before they could start building and repairing the air strip.

My sister's husband died from wounds he suffered in combat on 'D Day' and my first husband, Victor Martin, served in the Army Air Corps.

I remember the Japanese submarine shelling of Fort Stevens and the fire-bombing in Southern Oregon by the Japanese and our big airplanes and bombers flying over Portland and Vancouver.

Looking back at my high school graduation class, most all the boys in the class served in the War and many did not come home. Some of those who did, were scarred for life."

Where did you and your husband work?

"Like I said, I worked at the Newberry Store in Portland when I was eighteen. During the War, I worked at the Vancouver Shipyards. In 1949 Al and I purchased a farm just south of Silverton. We grew over 500 acres of grass seed, and raised turkeys, sheep and grain. I was always confused that the Government would not let us feed our turkeys with the grain we raised on the farm. They made us buy the grain to feed them. It never made any sense to us. You know that turkey was one of the largest industries in Oregon. We sold them to a Co-Op until it went broke and we were out of the turkey business. Grass seed farming is the third largest agriculture crop in Oregon. There are over 500,000 acres of grass seed farmed in Oregon of which over 485,000 acres are grown right here in the Willamette Valley.

Oregon's weather of wet winters and warm summers makes it a great place to grow grass seed and the seed grown in Oregon is noted worldwide for its quality and used all around the world for landscaping, athletic fields, golf courses, parks, lawns and reseeding burned areas. I just read that grass seed farming in Oregon is a $500 million dollar industry and pumps economic activity of over $1.5 billion dollars.

Al died in 1960, just forty-nine years old. I was thirty-seven and left alone with five kids. I continued to operate the farm until I sold it to my son Jim and moved back to Silverton. I got a temporary job at Roth's Foodliner and worked there as a checker from 1965 until I retired in 1982."

What events in Oregon do you recall?

"During part of the sixth grade we still lived in Silverton and were studying Oregon history. We moved to California when Dad got a job that paid thirty-five cents and hour. The very small school in California was confusing because there was so many different nationalities. I was way behind them in my studies and instead of learning about Oregon, they were studying California history. Moving away from Silverton and Oregon was very hard for me as I was homesick for all my school friends.

I remember one of the awful Tillamook burn forest fires when I was ten. The smoke was so thick and you couldn't see. In order to see to get to school, us kids had to walk down the railroad tracks real close to the boxcars. The fire was a long way away, but the wind blew the smoke right into the Silverton hills. My grandpa told me about a big forest fire in 1865 that burnt over 988,000 acres in the Silverton area. Because of that, and logging, which was big in Silverton, Dad said that many men volunteered to help fight the fire. The rest were very concerned if something like it could happen to the forest and remaining old growth timber in our area.

Evidently Dad said, the fire started in August 1933 from a spark from a gas powered engine and the devastating fire destroyed old growth trees, and turned the forest into wasteland. Being interested in logging and its history I've read that a series of large forest fires continued through 1951 burning over 355,000 acres. The fires caused the logging industry to stop. Wild animals of all kinds died for lack of natural food. The Rivers and creeks were full of dirt and debris and the seed cones to naturally re-seed the forest were burned up in the fires.

Since the fires, the forest has been reforested with the help of volunteers and professional tree planters. In fact, Oregon voters passed a constitutional amendment in 1948 that authorized $12 million dollars in bonds to pay for the work which began in 1949 and over 12 million seedlings have been planted.

Another thing I remember is the awful news of Governor Snell and his group being killed in a plane crash in October of 1947. We met Governor Snell several times as he was very interested in logging and was an avid hunter and fisherman. We first heard on our radio that the airplane he was on was missing and overdue in southeast Oregon. The newspapers had many articles about it. It seems that the Governor, Robert Farrell, the Secretary of State of Oregon, and the President of the Oregon Senate, Marshall Cornett were flying to a ranch near Klamath Falls to hunt deer. It took several days to find the wreckage of the plane which was located in very rugged terrain. All aboard, including the pilot, Cliff Hogue were killed. The logging industry lost a good friend as he was deeply interested in protecting and saving Oregon forests."

What do you love about Oregon?
"Everything!!! The beauty of it, the forest I can see from my kitchen window each morning; Silver Creek and Silver Creek Falls, the beauty of the Cascade Mountains and Mt. Hood and Mt. Jefferson; the green grass. I love the beauty of the Oregon coast and beaches though I don't get to see them anymore. I love the mild weather here and the people. Speaking of people, from my first day working at the Newberry Store in Portland to the day I retired from Roth's, I really enjoyed waiting on people. The work at the shipyard was very boring compared to meeting people. I guess I'm what they call a 'people person'. Most importantly, all of my kids except one, are living nearby."

Authors Note: Indeed she is a "people person". I don't think she's ever met a stranger or ever will."

What milestones do you reflect on?
– "My memories of grade school.
– Working in the shipyards.
– High School in Portland.
– Raising my kids, almost by myself in Oregon.
– Living and working on our farm.
– The history of the Thomas and Mazingo families that helped
    make Oregon what it is.
– Being blessed to live in Oregon."

*"–the longer I live,
the more beautiful life becomes."*
— Frank Lloyd Wright, 1869-1959

KATHERINE SCHWABAUER

Born August 1, 1903
Salem, Oregon

*"the first hundred years
are the hardest."*
— Katherine Schwabauer

When I mentioned to our next door neighbor about me writing this book, she told me about one of her friends who is one hundred and five years old and that I may want to include her story in it. She further explained that Katherine's next door neighbor, Tricia Campbell, constantly looks after her and takes her to doctors appointments.

Calling Tricia the next day, I explained what this book was about and asked if she thought Katherine would be interested in telling the story of herself and family. Tricia said 'by all means. Katherine likes to remember her childhood and Salem history".

Driving to her home in northeast Salem on a beautiful spring day in May 2009, I mentioned to my wife that this area of town was *'my old stomping grounds'. I lived just a couple of blocks from Katherine and that I was sure I delivered her the evening Salem newspaper when I was a kid.*

Tricia greeted us as we got out of our car and told us that Katherine had received a good report from her doctor that morning and she was waiting for us. Walking up to her white-stucco Spanish style home we noticed the many flowers and plants growing in the small garden in the front of her home. You could tell that she had spent a lot of time over the years planting and caring for them. Tricia confirmed our suspicions telling us that when Katherine was younger, she spent days and hours, often working from day break to dark, tending her garden, planting and weeding but now she leaves that work to others but always makes suggestions and offers ideas.

Tricia further explained that Katherine lives by herself. Until recently she climbed the fourteen stairs to her bedroom each night alone. Now she needs assistance by Tricia for her to navigate the steep stairway each night. Now she can't understand why she isn't allowed to do her laundry in the basement. For her safety, she wears a 'medical alert around her small, weathered neck.

Entering the small home, I noticed the neat living room with wall-to-wall pictures of people. Tricia explained they were her extended family and that everyone calls Katherine, Grandma. Katherine was sitting in a reclining chair in her kitchen 'nook' finishing a snack of French fries and lemonade.

As Tricia introduced us, Katherine looked up with her blue, twinkling eyes. Shaking her aged hand, she had a firm grip and a very pleasant and friendly smile on an oval shaped face. I was amazed that at her age, her full head of hair had hardly any grey. It was neatly held in place in a neat bun with a white lace 'bun net' she had crocheted herself. Later, as we looked at black and white pictures of her life, I saw that since she was a little girl, she always wore her hair in a bun. She wears round, wire-rimmed glasses and is a little hard of hearing, but so far, "I don't wear hearing aids" she proudly explains.

Looking around the small nook and kitchen area, again with numerous family pictures, I couldn't help but notice many instructions for Katherine, each in very large print. A couple in particular telling her not to go up the stairs without Tricia's help. The doorway to the basement has a sign, "You are not to go down the stairs." One listed, in very large numbers, Tricia's telephone numbers.

Tricia explained to Katherine why we were visiting her and said that they had gone over the questions I would ask her. Katherine looked up at me with a friendly smile and said 'I don't remember anything today'. I told her, it's all right and we'd just like to talk with her and explained to her if she got tired, we would come back. She apologized saying, 'I'll try. With the help of Tricia reminding her of her life, the two hours we spent with her just seem to fly by.

What is the history of your family?

I really don't remember much about my early ancestors. I know both sides of my father's and mother's sides came out to Oregon on the Oregon Trail, but I don't know when. I think my father's side had lived in Jefferson City, Missouri and my mother's family had lived in Hugh Point, North Carolina.

Well, my family lived here in Salem area all their lives. My Father Walter D. Pugh was born in Salem in 1863 across Capitol Street where I was born forty years later. My mother was Jessie Hobson and was a bit younger than my Father. She was one of several children. She was raised in Stayton, Oregon and lived to be one hundred and two.

What is your earliest recollection of your family life?

"When I was young, we lived on Capitol Street in the Parrish House. We raised chickens and Dad had a horse and buggy for us to get around in. Salem was very small. It seemed that half of the stores were saloons and there were livery stables all over.

My sister Mildred and me had a great time as youngsters. We took turns feeding the chickens and horses. Mother taught us how to sew and crochet and how to cook. I never liked cooking and still don't.

When I started the first grade we moved to south Salem between 12th and 13th on Howard Street, near the Bush Park We had a good life and had fun playing together, but we were not allowed to go to the park as tramps lived in them.

My sister was very athletic and I was sickly as a child. When she came down with the measles, I think she just had one spot. I was broken out all over and sick for over a week. When we got sick, I was the one that got it the worst.

We were very fortunate that none of my family came down with the bad flu outbreak in 1918. It was awful and many people died in Salem and in Oregon. I remember hearing that they had to use a grade school in south Salem as a place to treat people."

Authors note: *According to the Oregon State Board of Health, over 48,000 cases of the Spanish flu with over 3.600 deaths were reported in Oregon from October 1918 until September 1920. In January 1920, over 200 homes were quarantined. The epidemic killed 50 million to 100 million people worldwide.*

Records from the Oregon Historical Society show that the first case of the Spanish flu in the Northwest was in September 1918 when a trainload of sick sailors from Philadelphia came to the Navy Yard in Puget Sound.

"One of my father's friend's sons come down with tuberculosis. They had to keep the youngster away from the rest of the family. My Father had a large, high wall tent he used when he camped fishing or hunting. Dad loaned the tent to his friend for the boy to live in. When the boy got well, they returned the tent. Dad was scared of bugs since the big flu outbreak and would not use the tent anymore. He thought 'TB bugs' were in it. My father set the tent up in our backyard to let it dry out and was planning on selling it. One morning I went outside to play with my sister and we saw all kinds of Lady Bugs crawling all over it. Screaming in fright at the sight of the 'TB bugs', I ran into the house, shouting that the 'TB bugs' were all over the tent. Dad calmly went outside and after seeing the sight, he set the tent on fire. We watched the imaginary 'TB bugs' burn up.

My mother and father owned a farm in Polk County and in the summer my sister and me would go to the farm with my Dad in horse and buggy. I remember playing in the soft soil and running through the fields. It was strange to us girls, but the horses would not drink the water at the farm. They would only drink at their barn or the horse watering place which was located at the west end of Willson Park on Cottage Street. It's still there and is now a flower fountain.

To keep our food cold, we had iceboxes. If I remember right, blocks of ice were delivered to our house once or twice a week by horse-drawn wagons. I loved watching the horses. They knew which house they should stop at for the Iceman to deliver the ice.

We used to get our milk delivered to our house during World War II. Gasoline was rationed so the dairy delivered the milk in horse drawn wagons or in their small delivery trucks that they had taken the motors out of. Like the horses used to deliver ice, the horses knew exactly where to stop at each house. If I remember right, they did that during the Depression.

For some reason, my father got a job in Redmond and we moved to a small house near the fairground there. I celebrated my sixteenth birthday in Redmond. Redmond was a pretty town with the beauty of the Sisters Mountains and Mount Jefferson off in the distance. I liked living there, but I missed my friends in Salem.

My father eventually became an architect and he designed the dome of the old Oregon Capitol Building, the old Salem City Hall with the clock tower and portions of the Thomas Kay Woolen Mill. He had an opportunity to be a protégé under an architect in New York, but his father refused to let him leave Oregon.

My father built the house next door were Trish and her family now live. My first husband also lived there until my father built this house.

Mother and Dad visited Arizona and fell in love with Spanish architecture. When they returned home, just after my twins were born, he built this house for us. (Alfred, her husband, the twins and Katherine.) He duplicated the houses he saw in Arizona and it was the first stucco house of its kind in Salem. I've lived here ever since. We used to go out to the State Hospital grounds and stand on a bridge that overlooked a real pretty garden. We took pictures of us girls standing on the bridge, looking at the flowers. We would then show the pictures to people and tell them it was our backyard.

I remember the day the Titanic sank. My father took it very hard. Often he would take me outside and step off the length of the ship to show me how big the Titanic was. It was real hard for me to realize that the Titanic could sink being that big and all.

My grandmother who lived by the Garfield School, had a beautiful flower garden with roses, irises, daisies, tulips, and flowering trees of all kind. Salem used to have a Cherry Festival and they would take Grandmother's flowers and give them to the queen. That made me mad. I thought they should either let the flowers grow or give them to me."

What do you remember about the weather?

"Oh, I don't know. The weather in Oregon is good. In the old days the river (Willamette) and Mill Creek down the street would flood each year. The only way we could get to the farm in Polk County, when it flooded, was by taking the train from Salem to West Salem. After they built the dams, we haven't had many floods since. There was one in 1996. Some people in Keizer had to leave their homes as they were afraid that a dike would break and flood Keizer.

One year in January we had real deep snow and Salem just seemed to stop for a couple of days.

I was working for the State of Oregon when the Columbus Day hurricane hit. We watched trees blow down and all kinds of debris flying through the air. I was able to walk home. Our street was full of blown down trees. Our side of the street had electricity but the eastside was out for three or four days after the storm. We were fortunate.

One of the main reasons I love Oregon is the weather. It's not to hot or cold, with mild winters and no big storms like they have back east."

What was school like? Did you graduate, Go to college?
"Oh I can't remember too much about school. There wasn't anything else to do but go to school, so I did, even being sick most of the time. I know I liked it and got good marks.

Except for one year of high school when we lived in Redmond, I went to school in Salem. I started the first grade at the Yew Park School, which was located on the corner of 13th and Missions streets in south Salem. When we moved to the house on Capitol Street (the Parrish House), I went to Garfield grade school, and Graduated in 1920 from the Salem Senior High School which was located where the downtown Macy's store is now.

When I went to Garfield, I could look out the second floor windows and see my grandfather's and grandmother's house, barn and the horses. Their house was located where the Lee Apartments are now. I got in trouble several times looking out the window, wishing I was riding the horse instead of going to school.

When I graduated High School, I went to work for my father for a short time and didn't go on to college contrary to the wishes of my parents. I didn't go on to college."

When did you see your first car? What kind of cars did you have? When did you first drive a car?

"Well, I've never driven a car. That's why everybody is alive. In my days, women usually didn't have cars. The menfolks owned cars and drove. The first car I remember was my father's. It was a Rambler, a real big one. It didn't have any front doors and no windshield. It was high off the ground and me and my sister had trouble getting into the back seat.

My mother was in a bad car accident and it scared me. When I had my twins, I walked all over Salem. When I rode in cars with them, I was very concerned about their safety.

My husband owned Rambler's and Fords and he always wanted me to learn how to drive."

How did World War I affect you or your family?

"I didn't have any brothers and my father was too old to serve. I was young when it started and 16, I think, when it ended. I know that many men from Salem went off to war and many did not return. Some of those who did were never the same. I remember the big Armistice Day parades in downtown Salem and celebrations in front of the Court House. My second husband, Oscar, served in the Marines but like others very seldom talked about his experience. It must have been awful."

How did prohibition affect you and your family?

"It really didn't bother us. Being young at the time, I didn't drink and over the years rarely did. It didn't have any affect on my Father's business and work. I do know it hurt many farmers in the Salem area that grew hops and grain. I think the law was stupid, as people either made their own liquor or bought it illegally. I've read that many people became alcoholics"

How did the Great Depression affect you and your family?

"We made it through it. I don't know why they call it "Great"? There was nothing "great" about it! We, my first husband Alfred

Montgomery and me, had twins in 1926. During most of the Depression he was out of work and we had no money and trying to raise the twins. Times were hard for us as it was for a lot of other people. Alfred worked at whatever jobs he could find, and the Civilian Conservation Corps but the pickings were slim.

My grandmother had a large farm and raised chickens, vegetables and fruits and helped us. The twins never went hungry and we seemed to have food. My father and mother were always ready to help us and others in need.

Mother would feed anyone coming to her door hungry. My father was always ready to help others and worked at whatever jobs he could get building and remodeling houses and businesses."

When and where did you meet your spouse?

"Well, I was married twice. I first married Alfred Montgomery in 1925. I almost died giving birth to our twins, daughter Nancy and son Jerry. They were born August 9, 1926. Nancy passed away in 1977 at the age of fifty-one. Jerry lived most of his adult life in Washington State. He passed away in 1987 at the age of sixty-one.

In those days, they didn't have all the fancy equipment they have today and they didn't know I was having twins. For nine months I was very sick, vomiting all the time. The only thing they gave me to eat was one quart of milk a day. I couldn't keep nothing else down. I don't know how I stayed alive. I remember one day my mother was canning peaches and I asked her for a bowl. She gave me a very small cup of them and I wanted a big bowl. She knew better, but gave me more, and right away I got real sick.

When the twins were born a nurse blurted out 'you've got one of each'. She asked me what I wanted and I said 'a girl' she said, 'you got one.' Then she asked Alfred what he wanted, he said 'a boy'. The nurse replied, 'you've got one too.'

Now I have six grandchildren, the oldest is 53 and the youngest is 42 and I have seven great-grandchildren. My extended family is my dear friend Tricia and her family. They all call me Grandma and I don't know what I would do without Tricia.

Alfred and I divorced in 1943. I married Oscar Schwabauer in 1953. We met when I was working for the State of Oregon. Oscar was born in 1896 in Idaho and passed away in 1986. We didn't have any children together. He was an incredibly generous man and was the only grandfather my grandchildren knew."

What do you remember about Pearl Harbor?

"We were having breakfast when the news of it came over our radio. At first I didn't know where Pearl Harbor was. We got out our World Atlas and found it and stayed glued to the radio for any news. The Salem area was a beehive of activity of men driving to the beach to stop the Japs from coming ashore in Oregon."

How did World War II affect you or your family?

"My Father, Alfred and Oscar were too old to serve. Both of them did help out as 'block wardens'. We grew Victory Gardens and saved all our tin cans, newspapers, cardboard and cooking grease. We couldn't get gas or tires for the car, so, we'd walk every day to work. Many times we had to wait at the railroad crossing at Chemeketa Street for trains loaded with soldiers leaning out the windows waving to us. Many mothers sent their son's off to war and many did not return. When we heard the news of the A bomb, we couldn't believe such a thing could be so destructive and on V-J day we celebrated the end of the war."

Did you work 'out of the home'? If so where?

"I worked at the Miller's Department store in Salem for a couple of years until my brother-in-law, who was an attorney in Albany, got me a job with the Oregon State Accident Commission in 1943 and I worked there until I retired in 1968. I enjoyed my work and my co-workers some of which have become long time friends."

What events in Oregon history do you recall?
"Oh my, in my lifetime there have been many important events. Recently, Mount St. Helens erupting, the Columbus Day storm, Oregon's 100ᵗʰ birthday; the assassination of President Kennedy, the flood and destruction of the town of Vanport; the deaths of Governors Patterson and Governor Snell, and the terrible Tillamook forest fires.

I really remember when the Oregon Capitol Building burned down in 1935. When we heard that is was on fire, we all (Alfred and my Mother and Father) walked down to watch it. My father took it real hard as he designed the dome. We stood watching the terrible sight. I remember the crackling sound as the building burned to the ground. Large embers from the fire fell all around us and on my hair, catching it on fire. Alfred quickly patted the fire out and continued to watch the destruction of the building.

Authors note: According to 'Salem online History' of the Salem Public Library, on April 25, 1935 a fire started in the basement of the east wing of the Capitol Building and quickly spread to piles of old records stored in wooden boxes. As a strong updraft in the hollow columns enclosing the dome's eight supporting steel lattice girders pulled the flames through the upper stories. The core of the building was rapidly engulfed in flames. The dome inverted and collapsed into its well. Despite efforts of the Salem Fire Department, the building could not be saved.

What do you love about Oregon?
"Oregon has been my home for over 100 years and I love everything about it. I've raised a wonderful family and have wonderful friends in Tricia and her family. My dear friend Hugh Hayes stops by every afternoon and brings me chicken strips, a salad and coffee for my dinner. When I was able to get outside more, Hugh used to pick me up every Friday at exactly 8:30 in the morning and take me grocery shopping."

What milestones do you reflect on?

"You know, I've lived through twenty-one presidents; two World Wars; the Great Depression; the hard times we have now, the Korean, Vietnam and Iraqi wars. I've seen our Country change from rural farming country to an industry world leader and power. I've seen the best of times, the good times and the not so good times some of which are:

– My life growing up as a girl with my parents, grandparents and my sister.
– The big thing they made of my 100th birthday.
– This house my father built for us.
– The birth of my twins and the time carrying them.
– The passing of Oscar, Nancy and Jerry.
– My family, grandchildren and great grandchildren.
– The horse and buggy and the fun on the farms.
– School and graduating high school.

I've been blessed to live in Salem and see it grow from a small faming town to a beautiful city."

*"a life of peace, purity and refinement
leads to calm and untroubled old age"*
— Cicero 106 BC

114

HUGH J. HAYES

Born August 1, 1914
Wallowa, Oregon

*"pleasure in the job
puts perfection to work."*
— Aristotle

It was by happenstance that I came to know Hugh. After I
took Katherine's picture, I mentioned to her and to her neighbor
Tricia that I was going to have an artist draw the pictures for
each chapter. When Tricia told me about Hugh, Katherine perked
right up. Tricia suggested that I talk with Hugh as he is quite an
artist in his own right. Showing me a pictorial map which Hugh
had illustrated for the Oregon Department of Forestry when he
worked there, I said that I would call Hugh. Tricia replied that
he'd be here any minute and that I would be able to meet and
talk with him.

Tricia went on saying that every day at 3:30PM Hugh brings
Katherine chicken wings and coffee for her dinner. Sure enough,

exactly at 3:30pm, Hugh shuffled up the sidewalk and came into Katherine's home. He went right to work opening the box of chicken, pouring the coffee into a china cup and serving Katherine. From the look on his small oval shaped face, he looked very pleased and proud that he was still able to help his friend of over fifty years. He explained that mutual friends of Katherine and her husband Oscar introduced them to Hugh and his wife Florence and that the two couples enjoyed many trips together to Reno and Las Vegas.

Hugh has lived in his northeast Salem home for over fifty years not far from Ed Lambert. When I mentioned Ed, Hugh said, "I've not had the pleasure of meeting Ed". When we drove into Hugh's driveway and parked behind his fairly new Pontiac, I noticed a push lawn mower next to the garage and thought to myself, man, at his age he mows his lawn with that.

Before we could ring the door-bell, Hugh opened the front door and welcomed us into his modest home. Making sure there was a place for my wife to sit, he motioned me to sit in a chair across from him.

Hugh is five foot five and weighs around one hundred forty pounds on a small framed body. He is slightly bent over at the waist and walks in quick shuffling steps. His very fine, snow white receding hair accents his ruddy colored high cheeks. He is a little hard of hearing but does not wear hearing-aids or eye-glasses. His dancing and friendly dark eyes twinkled when he recalled his life. He is one of those rare persons who always has a very friendly and warm smile on their faces.

Looking around the living room, I couldn't help notice numerous framed drawings Hugh had drawn, model airplanes, a scale model of Fort Clatsop, a sailing ship that Hugh said he'd carved out of a block of wood and a scale model of the Titanic all of which he had built from scratch. He took great pride, and rightfully so, in showing us his work. He beamed with equal pride when he told us that the watercolor and oil paintings were painted by his late wife.

The clutter, if you will, of his life's work is neatly arranged and he knows where everything is. 'A place for everything and everything in its place.'

He proudly showed me a bronze plaque that hangs prominently by the front door. He told me that he designed it. The distinctive plaque has the names of the men he served with in the 340 Engineer Battalion of the 6th Army. It also lists the six places the unit served in World War II from 1942-1945.

What is the history of your family?

"My Grandfather Hayes side of our family came from Ireland. He was a mixture of Irish, Scottish and English and was a shoe cobbler and harness maker. I don't remember when they came to the United States. My Father, James was born in Springfield, Illinois. They took the train from Springfield to The Dalles, Oregon in 1890 and by horse and buggy to the small town of Wallowa, Oregon in northeast Oregon. Granddad Hayes continued working mostly making harnesses for the ranchers in the area.

Let's see, my mother's side of the family came from Germany and settled in Baxter, Iowa. Her father, Thomas Vernon was a barber.

The Vernon family moved to San Francisco about the same time the Hayes came to Oregon. The family lived there until the big fire in 1906. After having lost everything they moved to Oregon where she met my father.

My mother and father were married in 1913 in Wallowa. There were 9 kids in our family, seven boys and two girls. I was the oldest born the same day World War I started. Lets see, there was Vernon, Bud, James, Tom, Jerry, Myrtle, Betty and Patrick. Six of us are still alive. Vernon, Bud and Jerry have passed away. My dad lived in Wallowa all his life. He worked in the woods as a logger, and as a wood cutter, selling fire wood. We lived about two miles from the town of Wallowa, Oregon. I don't remember when Dad passed away. My mother passed away in 1994."

What is your earliest recollection of your family life?

The town of Wallowa was very small. It had dirt streets that turned to mud when it rained. The sidewalks were made of wood planking. In the middle of winter, there were snow banks as high as the storefronts. It was a real primitive town in those days.

We lived way out in the country on Bear Creek southwest of Wallowa. With nine kids in our family, it was very crowded in our small log house we lived in at first. We lived in several places, some were very small and some were bigger, we had quite a house full.

All of us kids had our chores to do everyday. The girls helped mother with the cooking, sewing and housework. Us boys helped Dad cutting and stacking our firewood for the winter. One of my chores was milking two cows two times a day. Boy, I got to not like that job.

I lived there until 1933 when I was nineteen. Dad was out of work, so I joined the Civilian Conservation Corps."

What was school like? Did you graduate High School? Go to College?

"I went to the small grade school in Wallowa. There were very few in the first grade class. I was real scared and thought it was horrible. I'd never been to town much before, let alone be around so many kids. I hated it. Most of the kids were crying and not wanting to leave their mothers. I just wanted to go home. If I remember right, there were only twenty or so in the whole school. I had to walk 2 and a half miles or better to school. That was a long way for a six-year old kid going to the first grade. Being the oldest of the kids in our family, I had to take care of them when they started school. I remember, even as a little boy, I loved to draw things. When I got in the fourth grade, my teacher saw my drawings and encouraged me to draw. She started me on my love of drawing. All the teachers were very strict, especially in the first grade. I was used to being the boss of my brothers

118

and sisters. Now I was just one little kid with a bunch of other little, scared-to-death kids.

There were four grades in high school and I graduated from the Wallowa High School. I was center of the Wallowa High School football team. We got stomped on a lot. We didn't have many kids there, I think 27, so there weren't many to choose from. I didn't go to college. When I graduated high school, times were real tough due to the Great Depression."

When did you see your first car? When did you first drive one? What kind of cars did you have?

"The first car I saw as a Model T Ford in Wallowa. It was a rag roof with no side curtains. Most everyone in Wallowa only had horse-drawn buggies and wagons. I remember a car got stuck in the mud right in the middle of town. They had to get a couple of horses to pull it out. My dad had a horse and buggy and finally bought a Model A Ford.

The first car I drove was in 1938 when I was in the Civilian Conservation Corps. It was a Chevy pickup.

The first car I owned was a model A Ford Roadster and then Chevy's after World War II. I've had all kinds, Fords; Mercury's, Plymouths and my Pontiac. I still drive but not far from home, just to Katherine's, to Yoshikai school every day and to the other people I help."

Did anyone in your family serve in World War I?

"My dad's two brothers were in the Army. They both brought back a little of the French language.

My uncle, Myron Hayes, was on a troop ship off the Irish coast about eleven o'clock at night when it was torpedoed by a German Sub. He was down below in his bunk getting over the mumps. He got his cloths on and ran to the door and it was jammed by other guys who had fallen down. He climbed over the top of them and got in a lifeboat. His lifeboat got half way down the side of the ship and the ropes got stuck. They had to cut the ropes. His boat fell into the water right on top of another lifeboat. Most of the guys drowned and they lost a lot of soldiers. Later on the next morning, they were picked up by another ship. That was the only thing he talked about. Both my uncles didn't say much about the War."

Prohibition 1920-1933, how did it affect you or your family?

"I was real young when it started. It didn't affect my family at all. But there were people in the Wallowa area that made their own whisky. Dad said that there were stills all over the place in the forest. I never saw one, but they were there."

How did the Great Depression affect you and your family?

"Oh yeah, I remember it. We lived in Wallowa and it was pretty rough goin'. Not much activity or work and it affected most all the people in the area. My dad still worked cutting wood. We always had a big garden and had quite a lot of food. We had a couple of milk cows and beef cattle, chickens and eggs. We lived out in the sticks, so hungry people very seldom stopped by for something to eat. Mom always had something for those who did. Them times were hard on everybody"

When and where did you meet your wife?

"Well, I was engaged to be married to Marjorie Bach when World War II started up. She died from a kidney aliment when I was in the Yukon Territory, Canada and in Alaska. I was able to come to Salem on emergency leave. I had to wait three days at the airport in Canada before they could get a plane off the ground due to a big snowstorm. I flew on a DC-3 to Edmonton, Canada. There was no seats in it and the heating system went out and all the metal parts in the plane turned white with frost. I remember, every time the plane made a right turn, the outside door would fly open. Boy was it cold. I attended Majorie's funeral and was here for a couple of days and then I had to get back to my unit in Alaska.

After World War II when I came back from the Army, all the girls I knew were married, with kids. I was gone almost four years and all the girls were taken and scattered all over. About four years later after I got out of the Army, I met Florence Ruffner. She worked for the State Highway Department and I worked for the State Forestry Department. From time to time I would go to her office with drawings and had to go through her in order to see her boss. We dated for awhile and were married in 1949 at Vancouver, Washington She passed away in 1984. We were married for thirty-five years. We didn't have any kids. It was just us two and our art and drawings. She was quite an artist. She painted all those paintings you see there on the walls."

What do you remember about Pearl Harbor?
"I was living here in Salem. I had just gotten out of St. Joseph's Church and when I was driving home I heard the news on the radio in my car. I thought the attack was pretty sneaky. I heard that many farmers in the area packed up their guns and went to the beach to stop the Japs from invading. I thought it was stupid and still do that our country didn't get ready for the war. There was war goin' on it Europe and one in the Far East. We just sat back and did nothing except start a draft. If I remember right, the bill establishing the draft only passed Congress by one vote. If your neighbor's house on one side is on fire and the other neighbor on the other side is too, you get a hose out and protect your house. We didn't do that until it was too late. The next morning on Monday, I got my draft notice in the mail, I guess my mailman was patriotic."

Did you serve in World War II?
"Yes, as I said, I got my draft notice the next day after the bombing of Pearl Harbor. I first went to Fort Lewis in Washington. With my surveying and drawing experience I was assigned to the 340 Combat Engineer Battalion of the 6th Army. I was then sent to Fort Leonard Wood, Missouri training center. From

there I was sent back to the West Coast to the Vancouver Barracks. After that I went to Skagway, Alaska and on a narrow gage railroad to Whitehorse, Yukon Territory Canada and worked on the fourteen hundred mile 'Alcan Highway'. We lived in tents for sixteen and a half months. In the winter it was very cold with ice and snow on the outside of the tents and white frost everywhere inside it. In the summer, there was millions of big mosquitoes.

I started out as a Private, then to Corporal, Sergeant, Staff Sergeant and Master Sergeant. I had a chance to go to O.C.S. (Officers Candidate School) but I turned it down. I'd been with my guys for three and half years, they were my friends and I decided to stay with them. From the cold of Alaska I was sent to Camp Sutton, North Carolina and trained to go to Europe. At the last minute, I was sent back to Vancouver Barracks, Washington for a short time.

From there I went to San Diego and took a ship on a zig-zag course to the war in the South Pacific. A big blimp went ahead of us for the first day looking for Jap subs. After that we were on our own. It took thirty-one days to get to Australia. After we loaded supplies, we took the 'inland passage' and hid out for five days as the Japs were looking for us with subs and airplanes.

When it was all clear we went on to Darwin, Australia. It was blown off the face of the earth. The Japanese bombing raids had destroyed everything. Just flattened it. It was a mess. We cleaned up the mess, especially the airport.

We were there for a couple of months and headed to Port Morsby, New Guinea for supplies. One morning we woke up and found that the ship was heading the wrong direction. The ship got the wrong signals and we were heading directly into a Jap convoy.

We went up to Alandai, New Guinea, I was sent to make a map of the area with two other guys. That was the first time the Japs started shooting at us. It was sniper fire. We hid out for awhile and none of us was hit. We were there a short time and got ready for an invasion of Morotai Dutch East Indies.

We built the airstrips there sometimes under fire from the Japs. We were there for about four months and every night around seven there would be air raids. They dropped phosphorus bombs that exploded in the air and rained down white hot burning phosphorus on us. We had to jump into our foxholes. One morning we got up to go to chow and there was no food ready. The cooks had found that all the pots, pans and kettles had hundreds of tiny holes burned in them by the phosphorus.

We then went to the Philippines, to Luzon. There were over nine hundred ships unloading supplies. The next day after the troops had landed, General MacArthur and a bunch of officers waded out a ways in the ocean and then waded back to shore. There was all kinds of photographers taking their pictures but no ships in sight in the background.

We did all kinds of building and reconstructing and most evenings we'd be shelled by twelve inch Japs shells. Most of the time I had to go out ahead and draw pictures of the bridges that the Japs had destroyed. The pictures were used in repairing them. I also drew relief maps of the area.

In 1945 I came home. We landed in San Francisco. What a sight seeing the Golden Gate Bridge."

Authors note. When Hugh mentioned seeing the Golden Gate Bridge, he just beamed in delight.

What kind of employment?

"Let's see, after I graduated high school during the depression, there were no jobs so I joined the Civilian Conservation Corps in Wallowa. I worked building trails, roads, clearing brush and fighting forest fires. In my spare time I sketched the projects we did.

When the boss saw them, he immediately transferred me to the head office in Salem in 1936.

Authors note: *According to the National Association of Civilian Conservation Corps Alumni, 'the Civilian Conservation Corps, sometimes called Presidents Roosevelt's 'Tree Army' made significant contributions in Oregon from 1933 to 1942, working on forest fire fighting crews, building forest trails and roads and reclamation projects. In 1940 Oregon had 61 'CCC' camps throughout the State and over 2000 'CCC' workers working in Oregon's forest.*

If I remember right, the Oregon headquarters building for the 'CCC' operations in Oregon was constructed in 1936-1937 in Salem at 2600 State Street. In 1942 with the disbanding of the 'CCC', the headquarters building along with the rest of the 'CCC' compound was turned over to the Oregon Department of Forestry. From 1942 through, 2001 the building housed the Keep Oregon Green Association and various departments of the Department of Forestry and now houses the Oregon Forest History Center.

"Later in 1936, I got a job in Salem with Lou Amort Engineering Company. I did surveys and made the drawings up of house plans, fire guard stations around the state, shops and warehouses.

When I got out of the Army, I went to work for the Oregon Forestry Department and work there for thirty-two years retiring in 1977. I did surveying, made maps, and illustrating the Entomology Text Books for the Department of Forestry. I did about half the drawings in it. I had to use a magnifying glass to see the various bugs that I drew. Do you know that the Wood Borer, Western Pine Beetle and Bark Beetle are among the principal enemies of our forest?

The Oregon Department of Forestry is the agency in Oregon that performs many functions to do with the management, regulations and protection of the forests in Oregon. It's duties include fire prevention and protection; regulating forest practices; implementing the Oregon plan for Salmon; forest pest and disease detection and control; and managing state owned forest lands and many more that sustain our forests.

The engineers would draw the rough work and I'd have to re-draw them all over again. In 1959, Oregon's centennial year of statehood, I compiled and drew, a pictorial map called, *'Keep Oregon Green, The Beaver State'*. I've revised it many times over the years and millions of it have been printed, some of which were used as place mats in restaurants throughout Oregon. The map is filled with and surrounded by captioned illustrations related to the history, topography and recreational opportunities in the state. Prominently featured is a list of the Governors of Oregon. Copies of it are available through the Keep Oregon Green Association in Salem.

The Keep Oregon Green Association was founded in 1941 and conducted education and information to prevent forest fires. Smoky the Bear was a major character in it".

In 1993 I drew another map of Oregon called, *A tour of Oregon's Forest Treasures* with millions of them in circulation. I carved a map of Oregon and it hung in the Forestry exhibit at the Oregon State Fair for many years. One of the booklets I illustrated is available in the gift shop of the Forestry Center outside of Tillamook."

Authors note: *The detail, in every way, of both these maps of Hugh's is fantastic!!*

"Since I retired I keep busy. I drew a cartoon strip for a couple of magazines. It was called *'Rusty Scrapiron'* . In it I tried to educate the readers in forestry, hunting and fishing and safety in the woods. One of my favorites shows Rusty Scrapiron investigating a hunting shooting accident. One panel shows the shooting victim with an arrow sticking in his back. The next panel shows the shooter with an empty bow captioned, *"I didn't know it was loaded."* You know, most hunting accidental shootings are caused by guns that were not loaded.

For the last twenty-two years I spend one morning each week at the Yoshikia Elementary School in Salem. I help them with their drawings and show them some of mine. Just before I leave, I have one of the kids draw a small "C" or half circle. To the amazement of the kids, I proceed to draw a cartoon character. I get a real joy of helping them. I figure that my fourth grade teacher helped and encouraged me in my drawing. I should do the same."

What events in Oregon's history do you recall?
"The one hundredth birthday of Oregon and seeing the covered wagons when they arrived in Independence, Oregon. With me working for the Forestry Department I really remember the many large forest fires in Oregon. In those days, we worked day and night Saturdays and Sunday's fighting them. I remember the death of Governor Snell. He was real helpful in saving our forest."

What do you love about Oregon?
"Everything, The beauty of it, the people, and the warm climate. After spending time freezing in Alaska and Canada and sweltering in the heat of the South Pacific during the war, there's no place like it or better."

What milestones do you reflect on?
"Milestones, well let's see:
– Growing up in the small town of Wallowa with my family.
– My first day of school. I was scared to death and hated it.
– The encouragement of my fourth grade teacher. Without it, I
    don't know if I would have done what I've done.
– The death of my fiancé Majorie.
– The day my draft notice came, one day after Pearl Harbor.
– My time in the Army, I wouldn't take a million dollars for it,
    but I sure wouldn't want to do it again.

126

– When I first landed on Luzon, there was about five or six of us standing around in the hot sun when someone said, 'why don't you guys come over here and stand in the shade?' We had just walked over there when a Jap plane fired its machine guns right where we moved from. I can still see the shells landing kicking up the white sand.

– Another time, two of us were out surveying when we come upon a checkpoint. The guard on duty asked who we were and before we could answer he fired his rifle at us. One bullet smashed through the windshield of our Jeep and another one just barely missed the right side of my head.

– When we heard the news that the War was over, we didn't believe it and thought it was just a joke. When we found out it was true, we really celebrated.

– When we arrived in San Francisco Bay, I couldn't believe I was home finally. I kinda teared up a little. It was a sight I've never forgotten.

– My life with Florence and her passing was another milestone.

– I am also thankful for being able to use my God given talent doing what I love.

– I see my artwork all over Oregon."

> *"art is the desire of a man to express himself,*
> *to record the reaction of his personality,*
> *and to the world he lives in."*
> — Amy Lowell, 1874-1925

EPILOGUE

These eight native born Oregonians lived a total of 645 years in "Eden'. They were not famous nor were they rich, monetary wise. But indeed, they were rich in living lives which made Oregon great. I'm sure that without these people, the story of Oregon would be much different.

As we celebrate Oregon's one hundred and fiftieth birthday we should pause to thank people such as these and say, Thanks, Thanks for giving us a beautiful place to live and work.

As you have read their stories, you saw that each of them experienced joy and sorrow. Some suffered tragedies in their lives, but none of them every complained. As Katherine said, "I've seen the best of times, the good times and the not so good times."

Harry, Ruth (Babe), Edgar, Helen, Ed, Betty, Katherine and Hugh went quietly about their lives working in their careers and as stewards of the beauty of 'Eden'.

They benefited from the courage, and yes, ambition, of their ancestors who gave up good lives in the East and looked westward toward Oregon to make a better life for their families. Some braved the dangerous and sometimes uncharted wilds of the Oregon Trail in wagons the size of today's 'mini-van'. How many of us would do that today?

When they arrived in 'Eden' they had to eek out meager livings in sometimes hostile environments. Some had to clear their fields of old growth Douglas Firs six to eight feet in diameter.

'Land of the Empire builders' are the first words of *Oregon My Oregon*, Oregon's official state song. These people and those who came before them did not build empires of industry or monetary wealth. They built empires of caring and loving families.

The tenacity, strength and vision of the parents and grandparents was passed on to these eight who in turn passed it on to their children, nieces and nephews, grand and great grand kids.

Their accomplishments, however small, were big in giving to the people of Oregon, whether native or transplant, a wonderful and beautiful place to live and work. As the gold pioneer on top of the Oregon State Capital Building continues to look West, we must continue with him, looking west preserving our shared legacy to keep Oregon and its beauty for our successors to enjoy.

"whatever their accomplishments,
we are their treasurers."
— author unknown